GO FISHING FOR
SHARK

GRAEME PULLEN

The Oxford Illustrated Press,

The Oxford Illustrated Press

© Graeme Pullen, 1989

ISBN 0 946609 61 6

Published by:
The Oxford Illustrated Press Limited, Haynes Publishing Group,
Sparkford, Nr Yeovil, Somerset BA22 7JJ, England.

Haynes Publications Inc., 861 Lawrence Drive, Newbury Park, California
91320, USA.

Printed in England by:
J.H. Haynes & Co Limited, Sparkford, Nr Yeovil, Somerset.

British Library Cataloguing in Publication Data
Pullen, Graeme
    Go fishing for shark.
    1. Great Britain. Coastal waters. Sharks. Angling –
    Manuals
    I. Title
    799.1'431'0941
    ISBN 0-94660-961-6

Library of Congress Catalog Card Number
    89–80216

Other titles by the author
Fishing in the Isles of Scilly
Big Game Fishing: The Great Adventure
Ashford Adventure Holiday Guide
The Graeme Pullen Guide to Freshwater Baits
The Graeme Pullen Guide to Sea Fishing Baits
How to Catch Cod
How to Catch Trout
How to Catch Tench

Contents

Acknowledgements

To Mr Peter Green of the Central Fisheries Board for assistance with Irish shark fishing details.

To Mr J. Casey, NMFS Co-operative Shark Tagging Programme for invaluable information on shark tagging, operations and results.

To Mrs Beulah Davis for giving me an interview and information on my visit to the Natal Sharks Board, Durban, South Africa.

To Capt. Jim Taylor in the Florida Keys, and Capt. Luis Laje in the Azores, for being the best shark skippers I have ever fished with.

To Capt Mark Terpeney of the game boat *Spring Fever,* who allowed his boat to get damaged by a 376-lb bull shark I once caught off Palm Beach!

Finally to my old Adler Universal 200 manual typewriter, which has seen me through the last five books without breaking down. One day I'll go electric!

Dedication

To the next generation of shark
fishermen. That there may be
unpolluted oceans in which they
can enjoy the pursuit of sharks.

Introduction

There has always been within man a primeval fear of the shark; one that is evident even among those people who have never lived near, ventured onto, or fallen into, the sea. This fear one assumes came from earlier times, when we were very much the prey, rather than the somewhat destructive predator we have become today.

While we have evolved over millions of years, the shark has stayed virtually the same. While we have seen fantastic changes in climatic conditions on a global scale, changes that marked the extinction of the largest land carnivore, the Tyrannosaurus Rex, the shark survived all, unscathed, unchanged. It is a professional oceanic killing machine unmatched in animal life, which will remain unchanged for many years to come. I hesitate to say for millions of years, because our own perpetual destruction and pollution of both land and sea is having a detrimental effect on all forms of life, including the various species of shark. For while they may be viewed as the most efficient survival killing machines nature has ever invented, they have to eat something and as commercial overfishing coupled with increased mutation-inducing pollutants decreases the number of fish on which they can feed, they too obviously suffer. It is quite possible that our grandchildren will not see some of the sea species we find today.

When you see a report on a pollution incident, it is after the incident has occurred. The tendency in our Western society has been for many cases to be understated, or even hushed up for fear of those responsible being identified. Here in Britain we are responsible so say the Scandinavian countries, for sulphur emissions being carried over the North Sea to fall as acid rain on the European forests. That more and more trees are dying is obvious. Each season I ski the alpine slopes of Austria, and note with sadness the drooping branches or wood carcasses standing stark against the white backdrop. As pure as the driven snow? Even that virgin white blanket has its share of pollutants whisked across the globe by the jet streams at high levels. Who needs the fear of the atomic bomb now that a nuclear plant that blows up thousands of miles away sends radioactive fallout onto your soil? It infects *your* grass which *your* sheep eat, and which is passed into the body via the bloodstream of *your* lamb. Even the manure from a sheep eating infected grass is recycled back into the system. Radioactivity is here to stay. It is only we, as consumers of our own pollution, that pass on.

In the vast oceans of the world many species of fish have been found to have dangerously high levels of petroleum hydrocarbons in their flesh. PCBs as they are known, have been found in silver hake muscle tissue, from fish that live on the very edge of the continental shelf. It is believed that this musculature contamination is picked up by the fish in their early state near the coast and in shallow water. They migrate out to deeper water, but then other fish eat the contaminated hake. The chain of heavy metals, PCBs and cadmium are, like radioactivity, here to stay. If you throw your garbage in the rubbish bin you think that is the end of it, but of course the rubbish still has to be dumped somewhere. You merely forget about it. Out of sight, out of mind as the saying goes — which is quite ironic really; because most of the pollutants we emit into the rest of the world can't be seen, tasted or smelt.

The head-in-the-sand syndrome is one which we, as anglers, should not adopt. We should be aware of the environment in which we live, and be aware of how others may have a detrimental effect on us, the sea, and the creatures that live in the sea. In my opinion, pollution and the loss of species will increase. There are others who would say that it is probably already too late. The shark, that simple, efficient machine of the sea that has survived all the natural, climatic and evolutionary changes that nature could devise, over a period of millions of years, could still be wiped out by man's carelessness and indifference.

Sharks have been proved to be something of a phenomenon. Almost impervious to disease, some of their organs are complex in structure. In their liver, the fats contain a highly sophisticated defence substance. This battery of antibodies can fight or repel disease-producing viruses to an incredible extent. It has also been found by research that a fatlike substance called lipid is held in far greater quantities in the shark than in any other animal. It is like a defence stimulant, preventing the invasion or spread of disease—to such an extent that researchers have developed a serum extract from it which can act as an agent to reduce or delay cancer tumours. A few years back I was researching a story in Miami on Pfleuger's marine taxidermy, and was not surprised to find that the carcasses of many of the sharks they receive to be mounted are sent away to assist in this research against cancer.

It does seem ironic that while we are getting help from the shark in the development of a tumour-restricting stimulant against cancer, we are in exchange polluting the environment in which the shark lives. Cancer is high on the list of diseases which kill humans. This cancer is often produced as a result of our own pollution. Surely if we polluted the sea less, we could learn more from sharks and their strange disease-free metabolism that might help cancer research.

The shark, to me, is a very special fish. For those with a vivid imagination, they are a sort of Clint Eastwood of the ocean. They know no fear, and are the last survivors of prehistoric times. I admire and respect their survival in their harsh environment, and hope there will always be sharks around, both to keep the balance of nature, and to provide fishermen with a hard-fighting species to catch. They add that little extra spice to a fishing trip, in that you know subconsciously that a shark of your body weight is more powerful in the water than you are on land: if you stood on a jetty and tied yourself to a shark of equal weight, it would drag you off the end so easily you wouldn't believe it. Well, you would when the shark then turned round to take a bite out of you! They also grow very big, which in itself is an attraction to many anglers. The largest shark species known is now extinct, although a few avid enthusiasts of the rod still hold the belief that they are alive, and swimming the fathomless depths of our deepest oceans. Between 12 and 28 million years ago a shark roamed the Miocene seas that couldn't really be called a fish at all. From fossils pieced together it has been estimated that it could measure up to eighty feet in length, and swallow a small car with ease! Such mysteries are always needed in any branch of sport fishing, but never is it more exciting than when you slide a freshly hooked deadbait back into a chum slick, set the reel check and await results. It is then that you can allow that primeval fear to surge to the surface, allow yourself that little glimmer of hunting instinct that so many people who don't hunt or fish claim we can do without. Like the shark, how can you change an instinct for survival that is at the heart of evolution? Without activities like shooting and fishing we would have no outlet whatsoever for this surge of fear and adrenalin. When sharks are your quarry in an open boat on a vast ocean, when that evil-smelling concoction of rubby dubby or chum is oozing its message across the current, beckoning the ocean's killers to come and fight, you begin to feel the hairs on the back of your neck prickle. Was that a shark fin rolling through the wave top or just a seabird? Did you hear the reel check tick as the bait below was crunched between slicing jaws? You begin to realise that the role of hunter and hunted has suddenly changed. The moment you put blood, fish flesh or fish oil in the water you are placing an advertisement for trouble. You are walking that fine line between sportsman and lunatic. And people ask me why I go shark fishing! It's just man's outlet to hunt, and thank God there are still men about who can sample that adrenalin surge when the reel hits a screaming wail as the line departs!

About Sharks

Whether the shark fisherman gets an extra surge of excitement when his reel starts to scream, or whether he is simply re-enacting a scenario from prehistoric times, it is difficult to know. We, as humans in the 'hostile' environment of the sea, are bound to feel slightly ill at ease when we fish for shark. For we are not in fact hunting the shark. By placing large quantities of fish offal and blood in the water we are pretending to be a dead or dying fish, and asking the shark to come along and attack us. Obviously we hope to set a hook into that tough jaw and have a tremendous fight with the tackle we use, but we must still have a certain respect and fear for a species that has enjoyed undisputed power in the sea, and whose only enemy is man.

While you read glorified accounts of the battles of yesteryear, the angler today has a little more knowledge at his disposal. More is known about the behavioural and feeding patterns of most shark species, yet some are so dangerous, or rare, that little or nothing is known about them. The great white shark for instance, is the most feared shark of all time, yet it is highly unlikely to cause a single fatality in one year in most countries.

Once we enter the water, without the protection of the boat, then we lay ourselves wide open to the various stimulants a shark needs for a feeding attack. Some species require a lot of stimulus to get them in a feeding mood. Others, depending of course on how hungry they are, depend on very little in the way of scent, visual or electrical impulses to switch them on. Some species of shark will in certain circumstances attack a man. But those circumstances are so

Go Fishing for Shark

A shark can take a big bait without ripping it to shreds, as the stomach contents of this Indian Ocean Whitetip shark, landed by the author, reveal. Just one set of bite marks and a whole ten pound skipjack tuna slides down the hatch. The shark hit the tuna while they were engaged in a feeding frenzy on ocean driftbait.

coincidental that you could drift about for days in a tropical sea and never see a shark. Their most acute sense is smell, so stimulate that, shall we say, with a trickle of blood from a finger cut and you could have problems, for a hungry shark knows no fear, and will home in unerringly on the source of that smell. That such shark attacks do occur has been officially recorded, although in undeveloped countries many go unrecorded except by relatives or direct onlookers.

Sharks, contrary to popular opinion, do not kill just for the sake of it. They kill to eat. They need to eat to survive, just as we do, except that they can't go down to the local supermarket and get a frozen TV dinner to throw in the microwave. They have to go out and do the job themselves, and with competition from other sharks and scarcity of food, those that survive become very, very good at what they do. When a shark attack on a human occurs it is normally for one of four reasons: the human might have the misfortune to be around at the time when the shark is hungry and actively looking for food, i.e. early morning or late evening; he may be swimming outside the safety of shark nets that are put up to stop sharks coming into popular swimming areas; he may have a wound that stimulates the shark's sense of smell, or he may be splashing around like a wounded fish and so trigger a response in the shark's nervous system. He may of course be doing all four, which is when many attacks occur. Even so, taking the world population as a whole you are more likely to be hit by lightning than killed by a shark.

During the Second World War, when a lot of airmen were shot down and a lot of men were lost in ships torpedoed or bombed at sea, the figures needed looking at seriously. The US Navy, together with the Smithsonian Institute, kept a Shark Attack File which was international, and had on their books more than 1600 instances of attacks on man. Some took place in the middle of the ocean, but others were only yards from the safety of shore, and in water no more than three feet deep; from the file, 407 attacks occurred near shore.

It is not always the biggest shark that does the most damage. Many fatal attacks are by sharks of less than six or seven feet, and weighing a hundred pounds. It is the severity of the wounds, together with the shock experienced by the victim, that makes many attacks fatal. Some of the bites from sharks, even complete amputations, are so clean that the victim, under hospital conditions, is unlikely to die. A ten-year-old boy hit four times by a nine-foot silky shark along one of Florida's beaches needed 100 stitches to close his wounds, but still survived. But often attacks are in remote areas where the victim loses a lot of blood and goes into a state of shock from seeing the injuries.

Ship sinkings accounted for the greatest number of mass attacks by sharks during the Second World War. One of the worst mass attacks was after the sinking of the *Nova Scotia,* a British troopship which was transporting 900 men, 765 of whom were Italian prisoners of war, to a British prison in Durban, South Africa. A German submarine torpedoed her and many men suffered injuries as they were thrown into the water. Of the 900, only 192 survived the torpedo explosion and shark attacks. Another attack was on the survivors of the *USS Indianapolis.* This horrific mass attack lasted nearly five days and nights. Of the 1200 men aboard, 900 escaped when she sank, floating only with their lifebelts and of these only 315 survived the sharks; a grim reminder of the efficiency of the shark when enough stimulant is in the water.

Some 27 species have been singled out as dangerous to man, and in the water with a shark is not the place for acts of bravado. There is only one winner when you are in his element. If he has survived millions of years of ecological change, it is a sure thing that he can survive you. As far as a shark is concerned it's nothing personal . . . it's just that he's hungry!

If we respect the power they have hidden beneath that tough, abrasive hide, and if we honour the fact that we still maintain our place at the top of the ecological tree by that respect, then sharks will always swim the oceans. But if we mindlessly destroy, pollute and contaminate not just the ocean's ecology, but our own air as well, then the years we can go fishing for sharks will be numbered. I have a strange feeling that even if we continue to pollute the globe at the rate we are doing, that survival instinct of the shark will be stronger than ours. It will not be that there are no sharks left for us to catch. It will be that we have eradicated ourselves as a life form and will not be around to catch them!

Tackle to Use

The progress made by the manufacturers of fishing tackle over the last twenty years has been fantastic. If you look back over the last decade, that progress has been nothing short of monumental. The reason for this must surely be the popularity of the sport. If there weren't a lot of anglers, the need to rejuvenate old ideas and offer the consumer the latest technology would not exist. As it is, we as fishermen demand the very latest and greatest in fishing equipment that will put the fish on the end of the line even quicker. Rods, reels, lines and hooks have all advanced with the advent of the microchip age, and we will hopefully see the disappearance of those solid glass rods and heavy reels with braided lines.

I do find it a little sad though, as I was in at the end of that era, when the Cornish blue shark fishing was at its peak—and wooden boats with creaking hulls were used with chipped paint covered over with mackerel scales, and the red mizzen sail would flap against the sky. I remember seeing huge Hardy Fortuna reels being discussed on the quay by the shark anglers of the time, massive 14/0 hooks fingered with reverence as tactics were discussed in broad Cornish accents. I even remember some of the regular sharkers who booked the same skipper, boat, and week every year. One was a doctor who fished with his wife. Another was a German ballistics researcher whom I once had the misfortune to have on board the *Paula*. Then there was a man with 'KANE MANO' written on the back of his fishing jacket. I was impressed with the macho atmosphere of those early shark days. I've seen crowds gather at Banjo pier at the entrance to the Looe river, gasping as they tried to count the number of pennants fluttering from the boats as they bobbed across the swell outside Looe island, on their way to the weigh station. The 120-lb braided lines were then thought of as an absolute necessity in subduing those wicked monsters of the deep, that were reputed to eat small boys for breakfast.

Little did I realise then just how many sharks I would end up catching by the age of 35, but those were the 'real' days, when lever drags, kevlar and boron were all unheard of. Tagging was a game you played in the school playground, and kite lines something you tied your favourite kite to. Now, like others, I demand only the very latest in tackle and equipment. I would not use those heavy, clumsy and overrated tackles . . . yet I still miss those days! As one who loves reminiscing I find it difficult to erase them totally, while accepting the fact that those 'good old days' will never come again. While you are participating in it, it doesn't seem as though the present will ever become 'the good old days', though I guess in twenty or thirty years time I will be looking back nostalgically on the carbon, boron and kevlar and say those were the 'good old days' as well. I remember reading Fred J. Taylor's books on freshwater fishing. 'Never go back,' he said, 'It'll break your heart.' Like so many I have gone back, and it has broken my heart, but with a tube of araldite and a good shark run, it soon gets mended!

Shark fishing is a fairly rigorous exercise, and for that reason it is wise to take full advantage of the latest equipment the tackle manufacturers can offer.

Rods

Rods, no matter what you read about them, are instruments for cushioning the surges of a fighting fish, and for acting as a lever to gain you some slack line which then goes onto the reel. The search is always on for the lightest in weight, yet strongest in fighting power. To get both you have to go for space materials and construction, so for that reason I mention just two types of blank. For the heavy

Tackle to Use

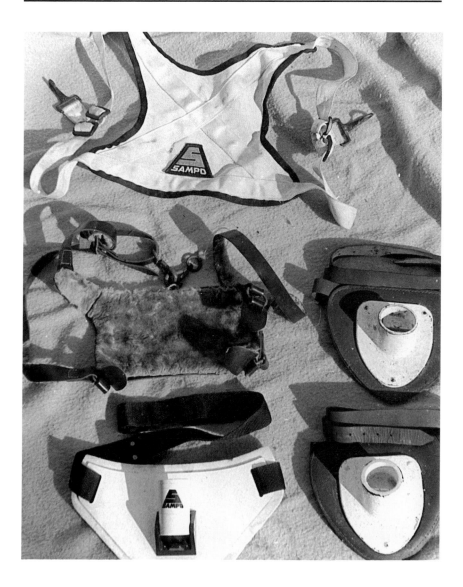

Some items to make a stand-up fight with a shark a little more bearable. Top is the lightweight Sampo clip on shoulder harness, ideal for line classes of up to 30 lb test. Below is a cheaper Efgeeco model to which the author has added a padded backpiece. At the bottom of the picture is a Sampo rigid butt pad with swivel gimble for the rod butt. The two triangular pads on the right are standard Efgeeco butt pads that the author has drilled and fitted a cross-pin into to act as a gimble.

sharks of above 200 lb in weight I would use only one make, and that's a Fenwick. It is American, but it has the reliability that a shark angler needs. It will probably break eventually, when stressed other than on a fish, but I personally have never had one break, nor have I ever heard of one breaking. They incorporate a 'helical bias graphite construction' in their new blanks, and it is a revolutionary new change in graphite rod construction. For years, the problem has been to develop a graphite rod without using glass scrim, those thinly woven fibres used to give hoop strength. Because of its lighter weight, graphite scrim is desirable, but the fibres tend to cut into themselves. When a blank is bent, although it is initially circular, it ovals under pressure, creating a weak spot. Fenwick's new MHG 111 is a continuous graphite material that can be rolled in both hoop and warp directions. This decreases rod weight, but makes the blank tremendously strong, especially in the tip. For this reason the best of the heavy-duty blanks, which I would specify as being for line classes of 50-lb, 80-lb and 130-lb test, the following models are best: The RT6350 is a 50-lb test blank, 63 inches long and only $11^1/8$ ounces in weight. The RT6680 is the 80-lb class blank. At 66 inches and only 15 ounces it really is the most powerful blank a normal man can use comfortably. At the top of the heavyweight range is the RT66130, 66 inches long and $22^3/4$ ounces in weight. These are unferruled, one-piece blanks available in black or white and are standard glass blanks. You can fit them with either a curved butt for extra leverage, or a straight butt, but on no account use wood butts. There is only one manufacturer of top butts and that is Aftco, who supply both types.

Remember that with heavier sharks these rods will soak up a lot more punishment than light-tackle small sharks. Moving down to the 15–30-lb tackle class range, you can also use the Fenwick series. They run these blanks down to 6-lb test class, or you can go to the British-made blank in the shape of the North-Western carbon/kevlar boat rods. They run a series of built rods in the 12, 20 and 30-lb range fitted with Fuji BNHG rings, a duplon handle, and with an overall length of 8 feet. They also market a 30-lb boat rod fitted with Aftco rollers of the same length. I would say this latter model is best suited to most European sharking. For the angler who wants real light-tackle fun, he should move to their 9 ft 6 in 4–8 ounce uptider model. The material used is a mixture of carbon, kevlar and glass, and although longer, you get a tremendous tip action, with plenty of backbone in the lower section. Without a doubt this material mixture makes for a good light sharking rod that is a pleasure to use.

I should mention for anglers purchasing their own blanks and fitting them up themselves that it has been scientifically proven that roller ring guides produce a fraction of the line wear experienced by other types of 'static' rings. Aftco make superb roller ring guides, and if I had the choice I would put a full set on every boat rod I had. They require little maintenance, except a good rinse under a freshwater hose. Other than that you need only strip them down and re-oil about once a season. If you look after a set of Aftco rollers, they will look after your line quality. And the line is that slender thread that connects you to the shark!

Reels

A reel is an instrument for storing line, and allowing it to be taken or gained under pressure. Although there are many makes and models about, all of which can catch sharks, I shall mention only those which I know to be strong, reliable and trustworthy. The change to lever drags is now introducing smaller and smaller reels, giving the advantage of this system while using light tackle. The leaders in this field must surely be Shimano, who have used their technology from the cycle industry to produce tip-top reels that are a real pleasure to use.

Let's start with the big, bruising sharks from warm temperate and tropical waters. Line diameter and capacity are of prime importance when you slap the steel into a shark weighing more than 500 lb. There is no point in messing around with a 35-lb livebait in 200 feet of water if your snap swivel links you to 12-lb test. The bait is liable to break that on the way down! For lines of 130-lb class I advise the trusty Penn International lever drag reel. They have been tried and tested for so many years on big fish that I have every confidence when using

Go Fishing for Shark

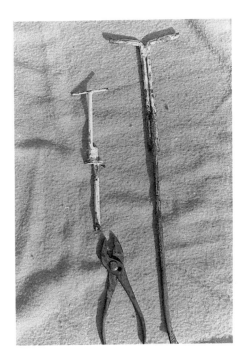

Unhooking implements. In the bottom are heavy pliers for jaw hooked sharks, a welded T-bar about ten inches long, and another T-bar of two feet long. Any hooks that cannot be reached with the 24 in. bar should either be extracted later when the shark is very dead, or the trace cut and the shark tagged and returned.

one. They are expensive as an initial outlay, admittedly, but provided you look after them you are looking at twenty or thirty years of good service, and you can probably sell it in the end for more than you paid for it! The best place to buy them is in the United States where they are reasonably priced. There probably isn't a shark swimming that couldn't be landed on a Penn International 130, so try one out if you are after the monsters.

For big sharks, but with a little more sport, you can drop to the Shimano 80 wide and 50 wide models. These reels, called the Triton Trolling series, feature the most advanced drag system ever invented, an exclusive ball-bearing titanium drag. It provides more drag surface area at all settings, and is really silky smooth. The only problem I have had was with a TLD20 that I submerged in a bucket of fresh water after a week's sharking, to clean off the salt. Water droplets got inside, and the drag began to judder erratically. I heard of a way to alleviate this problem from Norman Message, who fishes the wrecks off Eastbourne. He had the same problem, so took his reel apart, washed it in fresh water and dried it with a hair dryer. I did the same and it is now in perfect working order. It is a simple tip, but important—the idea of a lever drag is to give line to a running fish smoothly, not in jerks.

For big sharks on medium-weight tackle, the Shimano 80 wide and 50 wide models are hard to beat. For UK fishing, and generally sharking in European waters, I see little point in going heavier than 30-lb class outfits. In this category you can use either a Penn International, but I still honestly prefer the Shimano lever drags that have such a superb power range under pressure, which is important if you like to fight a fish hard, as I do.

There is a tendency with all reel manufacturers to offer more and more line capacity in their products. This comes from the popularity of light-tackle fishing, where you have to think seriously about getting as much line on the spool as possible. However, most anglers have no idea of the adverse effect the friction of water has on a long length of line being dragged through it. You can more than treble the reel's drag pressure at the point where the water pressure is greatest, so the more line you have out, the more chance of it breaking through water pressure friction, rather that the reel's drag. In fact the USA light-tackle specialists who hunt the ocean waters for big fish even admit to having been broken by a running fish when the line is in free spool. The roller ring company Aftco, with Bill Shedd, have evaluated this properly and given facts and figures from extensive tests. The results are startling, and you shouldn't worry too much about massive line capacity of 1000 yards etc. If it's under water drag pressure you can break 30-lb line with just 300 yards out. If you fish porbeagles, mako or thresher do not drop below 30-lb test unless you are experienced, and/or can afford to break big fish off. If you fish big blues, then not only does the 30-lb reel suffice, but you can drop to 20-lb, 16-lb or even 12-lb test. I once took a blue on 4-lb test above the British record but didn't bother claiming it. Americans call this light tackle 'stunt fishing', and I only did it for experience. Believe me it really is almost 'idiot-proof' provided you are prepared to wait around for ages barely pressurising the fish. With 20-lb line, however, you can let that fish know you are there, get a super scrap, and yet still take a big blue on such tackle.

Go Fishing for Shark

A good shark on, and the author starts the battle by standing up and clipping a Sampo shoulder harness to the reel. This takes the strain off the forearms and spreads the pressure over the back. Part of the fun of UK sharking is to fight the fish without the aid of a fighting chair.

Tackle to Use

There is only one light tackle reel to use and that's the Shimano TLD 20, with that silky smooth lever drag. The largest U.K./Irish blue I have so far taken on it weighed 95 lb, and was tagged and returned alive. For the 12 and 16-lb test category, I have used the Ryobi S320, which is a star drag reel. It has not let me down, and has a smooth drag. If you can afford a Shimano set of reels then get them, but for a reasonably priced lightweight star drag reel, this Ryobi S320 should do the trick, and catch good fish too. My biggest fish on it to date, other than sharks, is a 77-lb 9-oz sunfish taken from the surface on a tiny piece of mackerel fished on a 1/0 Partridge beak hook. The S320 is corrosion-resistant due to its all-carbon construction. It has a fast retrieve ratio which is another point in its favour. I still occasionally use a couple of old Mitchell 624 multipliers with metal spools. I have taken blues to 99 lb on them, and although now outdated by the modern, lightweight lever drag reels, they represent good value for money, and are so hardy if looked after properly, they will last for years.

I see no reason to mention reels suitable for lines of less than 12-lb class, although one other can be used for British sharking. The Policansky reels are lightweight lever drag reels from South Africa, and I have had two so far. Both had spools that exploded, and in one case the entire reel disintegrated! As you can gather I don't use them now, but they are undoubtedly alright to use in lighter line categories for small sharks. If you fish the real 'skinny water' in hot climes then the Abu Cardinal series of stern drag fixed spools are great for the job. They are smooth and can be used on the flats for sharks of 30 lb and over. Even then I seldom drop below 12-lb test, as often you have to put up with the line running over sunken mangrove, coral rocks and sea grasses, any of which are bound to weaken a line. If your favourite reel is a multiplier, then both Shimano and Ryobi offer freshwater bass-style multiplier casting reels that can take a reasonable capacity of 12-lb test line.

Maintenance of any reel is important, and after each session at sea they should be washed down in fresh water. A tip here is not to blast water at your reel from a high-pressure hose. All this does is to drive any salt particles deeper inside the reel, where it can eat away and do untold damage. It is better to sluice it down carefully, then after allowing it to dry, treat it with Superlube aerosol oil. This is the best lubricant to use and comes in several forms. There is the regular aerosol spray can, to which you can apply a narrow directional nozzle to get into those out-of-the-way places. I give mine an outside spray as well as this protects any new moisture from damaging it. When you have to take the reel apart for a full servicing strip-down, there is Superlube grease which comes in a tube. Finally there is a tiny hypodermic-type applicator that the angler can clip to a pocket. A gentle squeeze can put the lube just where you want it without messing up your hands and thus tainting your bait. The lube in all cases is Teflon based, and is honestly the best I have come across.

Lines

There are more makes of line than I would care to list, and all will catch sharks, but some are better than others. Personally I wouldn't use dacron in any form. Referred to in the commercial angling fraternity as 'Co-op string', it seems to snap at any moment and for no apparent reason. I have seen this happen so many times, and heard of it from other anglers, that I now exclusively use mono. The only braided line that I did use, and have only praise for, is the old 'Searanger' 55-lb braided in green. It was amazing. I must have had two spools of it that I sharked with for eight years, then gave it to some young friends just starting out. I think they've still got it, and are still catching sharks.

The mono man, and that means nearly all of us, needs a line he personally has faith in. I use Ande line almost exclusively, and have had no problems with it at all. It comes in regular and tournament strengths, the latter guaranteed to break under the manufacturer's stated breaking strains—essential if you are out 'pot-hunting' for a world record. I use it with confidence on all my reels from 12-lb class right through to my 80 wide outfits. I also use the Berkley lines, another reliable product from the States with an incredible listing of world records behind it. I use the XT, Trilene and occasionally other makes like Maxima or Sylcast. In fresh water I swear by Maxima, even though it can deteriorate and start popping for no reason. Simply discard it and buy some more. If I had to make just one choice in lines though, it would have to be Ande in green.

Hooks

I use two makes of hook, one is for the bigger shark, the other what I would term expendable, when I have to release a deeply hooked fish. There is no real recipe for preventing a deep hooking. It just depends on the way the sharks are taking on that occasion. If they have already fed well, the chances are good that you won't get any hook hold at all, as they can run with even a small bait held in the front of their mouth. This sounds a mite strange for a creature that has the reputation of being a killer, but it does happen. Then you can get the other extreme, when even early striking sees the trace disappear down the back of the throat. A hungry shark will not mess about chewing a bait to shreds. He will devour it whole, no matter how large. I have evidence of this from large bonitos that I have seen taken from the stomachs of sharks caught in the Indian Ocean. They were 150-lb whitetip sharks, and the fish in their stomachs were 20-lb bonito (skipjack tuna). Yet those tuna had only a couple of slices down their flanks, and were otherwise undamaged by a shark that could have fined them down like a shredding machine. When a shark is really switched on he will grab a prey, then in a series of convulsive movements, throw it straight down the back of his throat. I have even had relatively small blues with whole mackerel inside them, and I have seen the same in porbeagles.

The length of time before you set the hook can actually be quite short—between twenty and thirty seconds. That goes for a tiger shark eating a 25-lb amberjack, or a blue taking a 2-lb mackerel. My experience is that fast shrieking runs are generally from smaller fish, while the slower run that you might not even see at the outset (maybe the float has disappeared and line is loose on the surface) is from a

Go Fishing for Shark

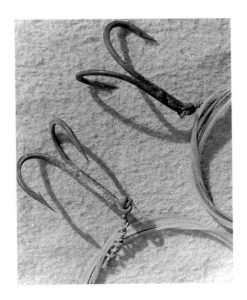

The author's rig for trolling baits for Porbeagle shark. A double hook system brazed or welded together, with three feet of steel trace, crimped via a barrel swivel to ten feet of heavy 300 lb nylon as the rubbing leader.

The standard three types of hooks used by the author. In the centre, the big 14/0 Seamaster made by Mustad is for big baits for Tiger shark or Mako. On the left the smaller 10/0 Partridge hooks for sharks in the UK like Blues. These can be straightened out rather than leaving the hook in the fish. On the right is the Porbeagle and Thresher rigs, a 10/0 Mustad Seamaster, suitable for medium sized baits of up to 1^1/2 lb mackerel. If using small livebaits for Thresher shark, you can use a much smaller hook like a 6/0 or 8/0 as the Thresher has a small mouth for its size.

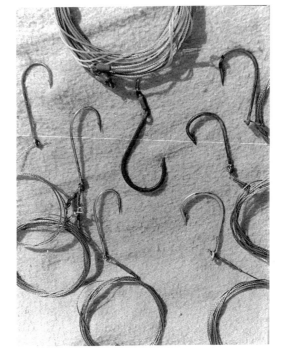

large fish. There's never a norm in any fishing, especially sharking. Just set the hook whenever you feel line is leaving the spool confidently enough. When this stage is reached you should not have to worry about the two pieces of equipment now taking the brunt of the fight—the hook and the leader.

To take the hook first, for big sharks—tiger, bull, hammerhead, porbeagle, thresher and mako—I would use only Mustads. The Seamaster range with the turned, offset point is perfect, and used in sizes from 8/0 to 12/0 will pull in a train. You can wire them up with every confidence that they will not snap or open out. I would suggest the following rough guide for each species, although as I have said, hook size should basically be determined by bait size. For tiger, bull or whitetip, perhaps a 14/0 would be suitable if you are fishing a big single-hook rig, or you can drop to a pair of 12/0s if you have a long bait, like a whole bonito or flank of 40 lb amberjack. For the medium range species like mako, porbeagle, hammerhead and dusky, use a 10/0 either singly or in tandem. Then again for blues and threshers which have quite small mouths, an 8/0 or 6/0 fished singly will be perfectly adequate.

Some anglers like to use the Mustad 7731 Sea Demon hook, as the point is not offset, but while this is important while trolling, it is not a problem when standard sharking. The offset point of the Seamaster will make any trolled bait spin, and if you are fishing a bait on a downrigger system, you cannot see this happening, until you either lose a shark on the strike, or see the coils of twisted line when you check your bait. If the latter occurs, either throw away the offending length of nylon or stream it out of the back of the boat with just a swivel on, nothing else, to let it untwist itself. When trolling you should use a Sea Demon which has a hookpoint parallel to the shank, a small factor that works in your favour.

If you fish thresher, blues or even small porbeagle that you wish to release easily then use the Mustad long shank 10/0. This is a wire hook that can be straightened out with pressure, on which a deep-hooked fish can easily be released. If you want to cut the wire then they are more acceptable to lose than the stronger Mustads. If you are on the flats, the smaller sharks will need correspondingly smaller hooks. I use Partridge, the strongest small hook in their range

25

Go Fishing for Shark

Graeme Pullen shows what the powerful pressure of a shark at boatside can do to a soft wire hook. This hook was almost straightened on a Blue that was held hard on the wire at the boat. Amazingly, he still landed the fish.

being the 'parrot-beak' pattern in sizes ranging from 1/0 to 6/0. They have an offset inturned point and are strong and sharp for hook penetration.

If you are a little worried that these hook sizes are too small for a shark, then simply tie one on the outfit you intend to use. Walk forty yards down the garden and get a friend to pull as hard with the rod as he can, while you walk back to see what is happening to the hook. The answer is nothing of course, the pressure exerted by the rod is only a few pounds. The real pressure comes when the fish is held hard by the wire, close to the boat and ready for either gaffing or releasing by cutting.

Another tip when trolling is to use a pair of Mustad hooks brazed together to aid in instant hookup. I had this done to a couple of rigs I made up. All you do is cut the eye off one hook and line up the angle you want between the two bends. Provided you get a neat braze or weld done it will remain strong, and both hooks will nearly always be in the back of the jaw, an ideal strong point.

As for wire, although I personally don't like it, I should mention single-strand piano wire. This is used extensively throughout the United States, but I have lost, and seen lost, many sharks on it. Only one kink is needed for a shark to create a weak spot and you've lost contact. It's fine in short three-foot lengths on the flats for smaller species, but I don't like it for the big sharks myself, and would prefer to use cabled wire leader any time. On no account use the plastic-coated wire, as a shark can strip this plastic/nylon coating straight off, ball it into a clump and have something to get those teeth working against. It can also deteriorate if you get nicks and cracks in the coating which you cannot see until it's too late. I have taken plenty of blues on it, but when I'm after something over 200 lb or so I will not use it. The first cabled wire I used was dinghy rigging wire. Seven strands of wire laid over another seven, it gives the biggest shark 49 strands of wire to chew through before you finally part company. This was very thick and I did experience a few dropped runs with it, but I had never had it break on me, nor have I ever heard of a fish being lost because it broke. I now use a cabled stainless steel wire that is finer, yet is sufficiently strong for me to have no worries of it parting. This is wire used for rigging as stays on radio masts, so check with your ironmonger who may be able to order you some. The best supply direct in the American fishing tackle shops is the cable wire marketed by Sevenstrand. This is really good wire, which I have never heard of breaking with a fish on. I have landed marlin on the Sevenstrand I use when I rig my marlin lures, so if it's good enough for them, it's good enough for sharks!

Crimps

Crimps are needed to make up your wire leaders when you attach a hook at one end and either put a swivel or make a double overhead loop at the other. I used to put swivels in the centre of any leaders I made up of 15 feet or less, but now I don't even put one on the leader end. There is a Sampo snap swivel on the reel's double line and this is sufficient to deter any line twist. You can make up your own crimps or sleeves from brass fuel pipe, sawing it to an inch or so then crushing it on the wire with crimping pliers. It's cheap, easy and will catch sharks. Or you can use the special sleeves for crimping made by Sevenstrand, who lead the field with their new design 'Double O' style. This enables the two pieces of wire, the main length and the tag end, to be crimped in separate channels of the crimp rather than crushed against each other. It is a design of importance primarily to the marlin fisherman who makes his leader up from 400-lb or heavier monofilament. Care must be taken not to crush or cut the mono leaders when crimping, and so the new Sevenstrand sleeve keeps the lengths separated.

I use only one sleeve crimped on the hook end, then cut off the wire about half an inch from the end of the sleeve. Then, using 12-lb line I whip tightly up and down this tag end until it is smooth to the touch and has no spiky end sticking out with which you can pierce a finger when handling a shark at close quarters. The tag end of this nylon is balled up by melting the nylon with a cigarette lighter. Do the same with the double loop at the other end and you have your shark trace. As for length, I make mine from twelve to fifteen feet long, which allows for the shark's rough hide to roll up and down during the ensuing fight. When you fish on the shallow flats for smaller species like bonnetheads, blacktips and nurse sharks you only need a short three-foot length of piano wire, or 'Marlinsteel' in about 30–50-lb breaking strain. With these traces I do crimp in a small barrel swivel, in case I am using a casting rod with a snap swivel attached.

Floats

As far as floats are concerned, different materials are affected differently by both the wind and the tide. I use just three materials—commercial net cork which I cut down to the size I require, balloons, round rather than long, and of course blocks of polystyrene. A float is designed not to be seen so much as to support a bait at a pre-determined depth. For that reason you don't want a

Tackle to Use

Three floats as used by the author. Left is a balloon and bottom is a cork with split to pinch the line into and a hole large enough to slide it up over the top of the rod. On the right is a commercial net float and standard cork, rigged on the author's no-tangle wire and swivel rig. Cork floats pull in the tide better than balloons which may drag a bait out of the slick by the action of the wind.

huge thing that creates so much drag resistance under water that you start getting dropped runs. A little larger than a big Jaffa orange is the size you need even for a 2-lb mackerel, while a balloon can be inflated to cover even the big bait category.

There are three ways to attach the different floats to the line. If you use cork or polystyrene blocks you enlarge a centre hole so that the line slides easily up and down, and either place a peg made of dowel inside to pinch the line at the right depth, or cut a couple of splits on the inside of the hole, into which you pinch it. Both methods require someone else either to slide the float up over the rod top or to let it slide back down the line onto the water when you play the shark in. This disallows any record, as nobody but the angler may touch the line until the wire leader can be grasped. A balloon can be attached to the line by a half-hitch, but when it gets near the rod top on the way in during a fight, someone has to cut off the balloon with a sharp

Go Fishing for Shark

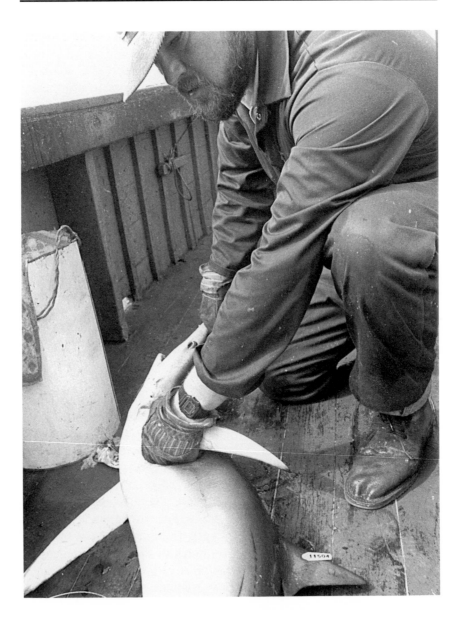

Shark skipper George Burgum gets to grips with a fish landed off the Tearacht rock. Make sure somebody holds the tail down, or grabs a pectoral fin firmly while unhooking and tagging even 40 lb sharks.

knife. This is not entirely conducive to relaxing the captor's heart rate! It is better to rig either of the materials on a boom with a swivel at one end through which the line is threaded, while a swivel at the other end allows you to use any float you want, simply by tying it to the swivel. With a balloon or any other float half-hitched to the reel line comes the added problem of line twist. The two swivels on my home made boom get rid of this, and allow free movement at both ends. They are easily constructed out of a piece of coathanger wire. You can stop the float either with a matchstick half-hitched round the line, a method I dislike for lines under 50-lb breaking strain, or with a bead and elastic band. You simply tie a knot in the band around the main line small enough to allow easy passage through the rings. I have yet to improve on this method, but doubtless somebody will one day make a purpose-built shark float.

Once you have the shark inside the boat you can either keep it for mounting, food, or other use, or return it complete with tagging and information recorded for research. While a small shark can be weighed on the boat, anything over a ton or so (2240 lbs) should be put on the scales on the shore. First you need to unhook the shark. With a mako that's simple—you don't! You unclip the trace at the snap swivel, throw it in the corner by the shark and clip on a new one. Makos are difficult, and I don't think they are really dead for at least an hour, no matter how many times you hit it. Makos are short on brains but big on heart, so take care. Docile, squirmy things like blues can be unhooked with the aid of a T-Bar disgorger. This is up to two feet long, and like me you will have to make it up yourself, as there is nothing on the market that is currently available for sharking. I have two, one for tope, about ten inches long, the other for shark, around two feet long. Inserted into the bend on the hook with a strong jar from your knee, you can get most hooks free, though you'll need some pressure! That done, I punch in the tag, write down the number, measure the shark and heave him back over the side.

Other Equipment

Something else which is not available to the shark angler is mincers. After years of being on the wrong end of a mincer I have perhaps half a dozen in my store. I still haven't found a manual model with a wide enough input to take a 1-lb mackerel in a gulp, and with a wide enough output to prevent clogging. Everyone suffers from skin clogging the holes that cut the fish up and there is only one way to clean them and that's a quick strip-down. You have no idea how many wing nuts and washers I've dropped down scuppers and bilges over the years! I have not found the perfect mincer yet. You simply have to try several types until you find one that suits, for a finely minced fish is the best way to get a good rubby trail, as it allows all the juices to come out. I have even taken a bag of fish that were supposedly 'washed out' out of the rubby sack, put them through the mincer and got another half hour's rubby dubby, with oil bubbles popping on the surface! The easiest way is to leave your bait, mackerel or even herring if you can get it, for at least a day. That way they soften and you can smash them up in a bin, using a piece of four-by-two timber. It doesn't get them as fine as a mincer, but it breaks them down enough to make a good trail.

The very best way is by letting the fish rot completely for about two days, just leaving them in a fish box covered with plastic or another box to prevent seagulls getting a free feast. Then don a pair of wellington boots, put on your oilskins and . . . get in the box with them! All you have to do is stamp them down as you would the finest grapes, but I promise you your wellie boots will never be quite the same again! This is a method I learned in the Azores from Capt. Luis Laje when we fished mako, and I have since used it to good effect elsewhere.

Mackerel make one of the best rubby dubby trails, but pilchards are better, provided of course you can get them. Herring run a close second, and as a final resort I would use pollock and coalfish. They deteriorate rapidly, but they simply do not have the oil content required. At a push they can work with pilchard oil, bran and oil added. When fishing out of Courtmacsherry with Brian Furphy of the *Security* for blues off the Oid Head, he brought out a special little

Tackle to Use

Other than mincing or stamping down the fish for rubby, use a steel drum and smash them up using a pickaxe handle. You can then add bran, oil and seawater to get a really gunky mess that the sharks love!

container. A grin split his face from ear to ear as he tipped the contents into the metal Guinness vat I was pounding mackerel into. 'Aaar . . . dis'll pop their eyes a bit!' he said. It was curry powder, so with a vindaloo special we fished all day, and still caught sharks. On another occasion with Brian I ran out of pilchard oil. He vowed to get some, and next morning I saw him pouring oil from a bottle into the tub. 'Where'd you get that Brian?' I asked. He nodded in the direction of the town. 'The supermarket.' It was a whole bottle of cooking oil he had poured in! I confess to being a little pessimistic about the drift that day, but, yes, we still caught shark! As for using scad for rubby, I have yet to meet a scad that I could get through a mincer, and that goes for all six of my models. They have an aluminium back, a cast-iron stomach, scales of mahogany and a skull—well the skull must be made of solid titanium! Forget scad, unless you let them go rotten for three months then run a dumper truck of breeze blocks over them. Stick to feathering for mackerel.

You need to ensure that you have enough bait for rubby dubby or chum. If the sharks are already close to the boat when you stop, if you have the wind over tide conditions, then you will catch with just half a bag of rubby over. More likely you are going to need a couple of full bags that will need changing about three times during the day. That's half a dustbinful, and mackerel are not very big when they've been minced down.

Let's assume you have about a quarter of a seven-stone fish box, and you want to go sharking. Take out just a dozen for hookbait and put them straight in a bucket of water to keep them fresh. You probably won't need a dozen, but it is better to err on the safe side. Mince up the others which might make about half what you thought you had. An old dustbin is ideal for keeping rubby in because it has that most treasured item, a lid! Put all the minced rubby in the bin, add some sea water, a cupful of pilchard oil—more if you can spare it—and stir round thoroughly, Mix in some sand, followed by as much bran as you want. You need to add more sea water to moisten the bran and spread the blood and oil throughout. Do not fill the bin over three-quarters full, because during the course of the night, sometimes earlier in hot weather, the bran will expand as it absorbs the blood, oil and sea water and will burst through the lid and ooze

Tackle to Use

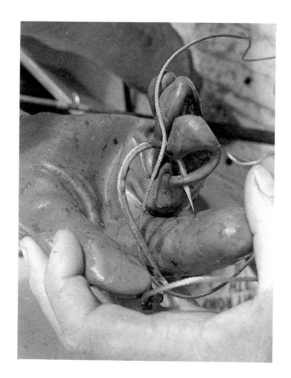

Danger always lurks close by when sharking. This was an incredibly lucky escape for one skipper who could have lost a couple of fingers. The shark was unhooked, tagged, and as it was heaved back over the gunnel, its tail got caught in the wire trace. This dragged the loose trace and hook right into the skipper's hand and the hook ripped into his gloves, cutting his fingers underneath. If he hadn't been wearing gloves there could have been a serious accident.

over the floor.

I start my drift with just one onion sack of rubby tied to the centre of the boat (outside, obviously!), and leave this in for half an hour. Then I tie a fresh bag up off the bow, moving the first one down near the stern. After about half an hour I tip out, remix and reload the first one, alternating every half hour. That keeps the slick strong, and, more important, constant. If you have plenty of rubby, put out an extra bag or so. You must shake each bag every five minutes or so to release fresh particles of oil and fish, otherwise they clog up. If you see a shark near the floats, or around the boat, you can fire him up by giving both bags a tremendous shaking, then waiting for things to happen. That usually gets a result inside ten minutes. Never tip a washed out bag over the side. The idea is to attract the sharks, not feed them up so much that they are gorged and won't take a hookbait.

Go Fishing for Shark

If you are intent on bringing a shark aboard for weighing and photographing, or want to bring it to shore for the same reason, you'll need a couple of gaffs and a tail rope, depending on the size of fish you are going after. Small blues and porbeagles can be dragged over the side on the wire alone, by one man, if they are under 100 lb in weight. Over that and you need a stout gaff. If you want to bring in something of 200 lb and up, you need a flying gaff. This is a large, preferably stainless steel, gaff head, which is detachable from a pole shaft of up to eight feet. This gaff head has an eyelet welded to it, through which you tie a rope. The other end of the rope is fixed to something secure like the stem of the fighting chair if the boat has one, or its mooring cleats. Thus, when the flying gaff is driven home, should the shark be extremely unhappy about the proceedings, the gaff pole is twisted loose, leaving the gaff held in position by the rope. If the shark in question happens to be a mako then it is almost a foregone conclusion that he is going to be thoroughly browned off with a gaff head in him and will spin and snap like crazy. This is why we don't want a fixed gaff pole, which can generally flail around and do somebody some damage.

I once took part in what can best be described as a mêlée with a mental mako. I was unfortunate enough to find my gaff head tangled in wire, mako and rope during this operation and received a smack on the back of the head from the gaff handle for my trouble. The mako also got away!

Techniques

Drifting

Few anglers realise the care that must be taken in order to give yourself the best chance of catching a shark. Despite the popular belief that you just stop the boat anywhere and throw a dead fish over the side with a hook in it, successful modern sharking must take into account the interaction of wind and tide. When you are fishing from a drifting boat these two factors remain of paramount importance. Each species of shark should have a different angle of approach and while most anglers leave such matters to the skipper, I prefer to make my own decisions and suggest to the skipper where to try and the method I wish to use. There are, however, two places around the British coastline where I would take the skipper's advice. One is off the north Devon and Cornish coast, fishing for porbeagles, generally out of Padstow. Those men do it most of the summer, and having a lot of light-line fanatics aboard are constantly looking for some huge pregnant female to claim as a record. In fact the record of most species are nearly always females in pup, but that's what makes records, so if you are a record-chaser you have to kill what may be part of the future shark population. The other place I would take the skipper's advice is off the back of the Isle of Wight, where Gosport shark skipper Ted Legge specialises in chasing the packs of porbeagles and big thresher sharks that inhabit the area. I have never had the honour of fishing with Ted in British waters, but his reputation for dedication is unsurpassed, and with a record of as many as 17 porbeagles in one day, few would dispute that he is the leading shark skipper of the last few years. Both these areas have set methods and areas where the sharks are likely to come, so you would be a fool not to take the boatman's advice on area and technique.

The standard method of approach for 'general' sharking, which covers broadly four species, the blue, mako, thresher and porbeagle, is by drifting. The boat is steamed out to wherever the likely area is, the engine stopped, and the vessel then drifts at the mercy of the wind and tide. You can easily do this, drop over a sack of rubby dubby, put out a shark line, and catch a shark. I've done it, so it does happen. I have also had sharks as soon as I have had the boat stop, without putting a rubby sack in the water. You tend to think the area is then heaving with sharks, but it is just that you are lucky enough to have stopped where a shark was swimming. He may even have been attracted by the throb of the boat's engines. However, if you spend any length of time pursuing these fish, you soon begin to appreciate that the more thought and time you put into approaching the fishing, the more reward you get from it.

Let me try to explain what happens when you set up a rubby dubby trail. The boat stops and you hang a bag of fish over the side. Immediately that fishy smell starts spreading away as the boat is moved along by either tide or wind or both. After about an hour, depending on the strength of the wind, you will have a smell lane stretching away from you of between a few hundred yards to a couple of miles. Sharks swimming across this smell trail are immediately stimulated and swim to wherever that smell is the strongest. They are drawn like a magnet to the boat, and on the way there we hope they will intercept our baits. That is the basis for all drifting techniques. But imagine that there is no such thing as tide. You are in the middle of a vast lake and the breeze is blowing from the north at force three. The boat then drifts directly south and the smell trail runs straight off the side. It's easy to get a picture of the trail, getting wider and deeper as it slowly sinks the farther the boat drifts. This is how it would be if there were no tide, but unfortunately there is, and it can either make or break a day's sharking. Imagine another scenario. You are in an

A typical British shark boat, ready to set a drift for shark. While drifting is the normal practice, the writer believes a chum trail from an anchored boat would result in the capture of a lot more Porbeagle and Thresher.

enormously wide river, moving along at maybe a knot or two. There is not a breath of wind and the surface of the water is glassy calm. The boat is drifted along at the pace of the water flow, and the rubby trail sinks slowly underneath the boat, possibly spreading behind slightly, but generally sinking down deep. Now put the two factors together, both wind and tide at the same time, and you begin to see the enormous combination of factors that can affect the area of distribution of the rubby trail. If you have a wind blowing the boat in a southerly direction, and the tide is running east to west, your drift will be diagonal, in a south-westerly direction.

There is also a third factor to be taken into account. The tidal flow will not be constant, and an ebb, flood and slack water will affect the trail distribution. Imagine that you are drifting in a southerly direction at slack water pushed by the wind. In an hour the flood tide will start and gain in strength until you drift in a curve to that south-westerly direction. After six hours it will be high water, which gives you slack and the wind, assuming it is still blowing from the same quarter, will push you directly south again. The ebb tide will start to run east, which will put the boat's drift in a south-easterly direction, so you can see that even during one day there will be three different directions that the boat will drift in. First to the south, then to the south-west and finally to the south-east. This is a scenario rarely experienced by anglers or tourists, simply because many of the charter boats will only give you about four hours of drifting and fishing time by the time they have reached the sharking grounds. When I am asked by a skipper to go out and show them how to approach modern sharking, or if I am asked to write a promotional feature article on them, then I request a full day to enable me to experience a drift through both tidal influences of ebb and flood. It means a very long day, but if they want me to catch them a shark, that's what we have to do.

I do quite a bit of big game fishing for marlin in tropical waters, and they are a lazy fish that only get switched on when stimulated by hunger, which puts them in the feeding mode. Most of the time they are found swimming with the ocean or tidal current, lazily tail-wagging their way along the surface. Their food is mackerel, bonito, small tuna and dolphin or dorado. All of these have a phenomenal turn of speed, which means a marlin has to have an even faster turn of speed to catch them. They use the wave power to add that extra impetus to their attack, and often take an artificial lure best when running the boat down the wave faces, rather than into them. In contrast it is believed that sharks swim into any current or tidal flow, their sideways head-swinging movement when swimming giving their olfactory or smell senses the best chances of locating food. I have no idea whether or not this is true, but I have heard it from enough fishermen to believe there must be something in it.

If the sharks feed into the tide, then the best thing your drifting boat can do is to drift against this tidal flow. This it can only do when the wind is in direct opposition to the tidal flow. Obviously this is a rare occurrence, but as long as the wind has at least some quarter of directional opposition to the tide, then the tide will take the rubby dubby trail away from the boat much better than either wind or tide alone. This is the perfect situation to be in. The sharks are supposed to swim into the tide, and the wind is holding the boat stationary against the tide, which is distributing the smell trail constantly and evenly. If you are fishing a south of England coast mark for instance, the ebb and flood direction of the tide will be roughly east to west and vice-versa. Therefore a southerly or northerly wind is going to push you across the tide. You need either an east or west wind, but remember it can't give you a good trail for ever. The tide, if it is flooding, will only run for six hours before becoming slack and running the other way!

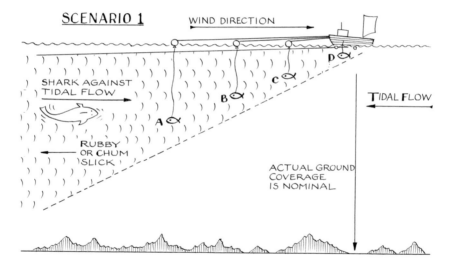

I therefore work on the assumption that I should time my trip to coincide with the tidal movement offshore (tide times differ from port to fishing ground, so consult your tidetable or check with the coastguard), but only if the wind is going to be against that tidal flow for the better part of six hours. Let's assume the perfect scenario, which doesn't happen often, but when it does you simply have to go for it. The flood tide starts to run from east to west at 9 am, and the wind is a straight westerly, force three, with a forecast to increase to five and move to southerly. You don't want to leave at 9 am because you may not reach the shark ground until 11 am and you will have missed the initial slack water low period, which is ideal as the westerly wind will push you in a straight line east until the first of the flood picks up. That enables you to get a start on a long trail, and you will then have a full seven hours with a straight wind against the tide trail. In theory of course you will get eight hours, as there is a period of slack water high that will still see the wind push you east. This situation must be acted upon whenever there is a wind against tide combination, from whatever direction the tidal flow is.

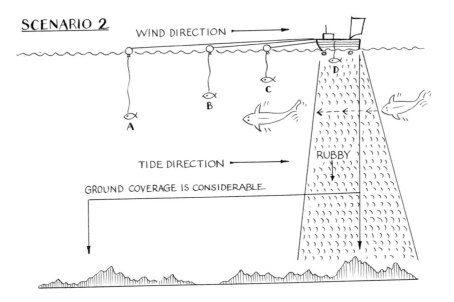

SCENARIO 2

WIND DIRECTION

TIDE DIRECTION

GROUND COVERAGE IS CONSIDERABLE

RUBBY

The worst conditions are wind with tide, because instead of being stretched out over a long shallow strip, the rubby trail will be drifting along underneath the boat, sinking towards the bottom. Another two considerations need to be taken into account. These are spring tides and neap tides. Springs are the bigger water mass movements so a strong tide will distribute the trail better. It also seems to activate all species of fish more, so if you are drifting way offshore you need as much tidal flow as you can get. While wind against tide is best, and wind with tide the worst, another bad time to drift offshore, is on a neap tide when there is no wind at all. Again the rubby trail will sink to the bottom, or balloon out in a big mushroom cloud for half a mile around the boat. When this happens the concentration of smell is not acute, but fairly even over a very large area. Therefore any shark entering this smell circle will not know where to locate the boat. What you want is a thin, narrow line of trail so that any shark crossing it will circle back, enter the trail and weave his way towards the strongest scent. The baits will also lie better in a wind against tide situation, tight in the path of the slick.

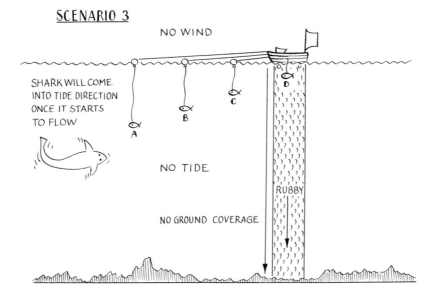

I'm not saying you cannot catch a shark in the worst conditions. I've done so, and I know that in fishing you can never keep to one particular theory for too long. But I have been very successful through abiding by these guidelines. You also have optional refinements that you can make, and which can have a bearing on whether or not you catch anything. If the boat has a large forward cabin then the wind can get behind this and push the boat along at an angle. Years ago, when the blue shark fishing industry out of Looe,

The author has a reputation for creating rubby dubby like a Cordon Bleu chef! Using wellies he gets in this 7 stone fish box of rotten pollock and stamps them into a pulp like grapes! This is far easier than mincing, and much quicker.

Cornwall, was in full swing, the boats had a stern mast with a mizzen sail fixed to it. This was to aid steering in rough weather, but it was also used on a shark drift to straighten the boat so that it was square, or beam-on to the wind, thus counteracting the effect the wind had on the forward cabin. If your boat has a mizzen sail, then use it to full effect. If it doesn't, try altering the rudder on full turn in either direction and see if it straightens the boat up. The more square you can get your boat to lie in the wind, the wider your rubby trail will be, and therefore the more chance you have of getting a shark take. In the perfect situation you have the rudder turned or the mizzen up, so the boat is square to the wind, and the wind is as near against the tide as you are going to get. If you use a mackerel, bran and pilchard oil mix for your chum trail you can easily see the slick away on the surface, and you will have your floats and baits out at different intervals in the slick.

So far I have mentioned the actual drift itself and the way it affects that rubby or chum trail. Now let's take a look beneath the surface. The strongest concentration of smell will be directly by the bags, and close to the boat. The farther away from the boat you get, the wider the trail gets, but the deeper it gets, and the weaker that concentration of smell will be. Sharks have phenomenal olfactory senses and need only a very slight smell to activate them into hunting mode. But not only does the slick grade itself out wider the farther it gets from the boat, but it sinks deeper as well. The trail near the boat—for say the first twenty yards—will be shallow if the wind and tide are strong. Therefore there is little point in putting a bait at ten fathoms only twenty yards from the boat. That bait will be well outside the slick and be missed by the sharks. Therefore the deepest set bait must be at the back of the trail, and then the next deepest, the next, and then the shallowest one set maybe twenty yards from the boat. This gives you the greatest spread of baits to locate a shark, and avoids what we call 'double baits' which inexperienced anglers get when they put all their baits at the same depth, and close together. A shark comes along, and before the reel has had time to shriek its warning, it has two baits. I know of an Irish specimen blue of 110 lb taken out from Achill Head in County Mayo that took three baits in short order. I believe it was Alan Hawkins, Colin Shaw and Bob

Go Fishing for Shark

Burchett, who must have thought for a minute they had been hit by a pack of killer blues! Of course any shark being fought by more than one angler cannot give a full account of itself, and is a credit to neither man. This is why correct spacing of baits is essential.

There is an exception to this rule, and it is by realising there has been a variation in factors acting on the boat's drift, that I change tactics to capitalise on these changes. Some anglers say it is all luck, but I have outfished as many as eight people at a time on a shark boat by knowing what has been going on. It got to the embarrassing point on one press trip to Courtmacsherry in southern Ireland, that I actually had to give another angling journalist from the north of England a run on my rod so that he didn't draw a blank! He refused all offers of a run until I had given three other anglers their first shark, and as a writer on fishing he was feeling the tongues wagging as to why he couldn't get a run when I had reels going all day. Finally

Most sharking is done over barren ground in deep water. While playing the waiting game for a shark run, you can have sport on light tackle with big Garfish, like this specimen held by the author, that are also attracted to the rubby dubby slick. An acrobatic fighter, they can also be used for bait when mackerel are scarce. Simply snap off the beak and you have a bait.

he gave in and sheepishly fought a fish on my 30-lb outfit, which at least gave him a fish.

One of the factors to be taken into account is this. If the wind speed increases to four or five, aside from being more than a little uncomfortable, it also means the boat is dragged fast and the trail stays very near the surface, sometimes no more than twenty feet deep when it is fifty yards from the boat. Therefore any bait set at more than thirty feet will be out of the slick, no matter how near or far it is put from the boat. Then you can afford to shorten up those outside deep baits often right up to ten feet, even though they may be 100 yards away. The sharks will be running shallow and therefore will intercept the distant bait first, almost every time. It is an advantage over your opposition in the boat, and one to remember. However you should also watch the float for signs of a take, rather than just listen to the reel, in order to minimise the chances of that 'double take'.

Another time when you must change from the standard pattern is when there is wind with the tide, or neap tide and no wind. The rubby trail will be ballooning out all round the boat in a fairly strong mixture so any shark patrolling will possibly miss the outside baits and simply home in on the bag under the boat, many times appearing right at the surface. I have even been lying on the stern near the rubby sack in a sharker's doze, only to be woken from slumber by the splashing as a big blue has ripped into the bag not three feet from my head! It certainly gives you a vivid picture of how quietly these creatures can sneak up on you, and is excellent for producing nightmares! When these conditions occur, you can pick up the most fish by simply sliding a float on your line about a fathom above the trace, and letting it sit about five yards from the boat. The old Cornish skippers used to swear that it would always be the inside line that went first. Another little trick I used was to keep a light rod tackled up with a shark trace clipped on, leaving it propped in a corner ready for instant baiting if I saw a shark cruising near the surface. Now what I do is to drop this bait over the stern, leave it out of gear with the reel check on, and set it just so the trace is out of sight. That makes it about fifteen feet deep. I have had many big blues like this, and possible more under the boat than on the distant line which is so popular with many anglers.

Go Fishing for Shark

If you are sharing a boat with strangers, you should ask them where they want to put their bait, and at what depth. This is a problem that is best sorted out before you start fishing, as there is always some greedy individual who will shallow his bait (or deepen it) to follow the pattern of the last run. All this does is increase the chances of a double bait. For myself I invariably use two rods, putting the outside line down very deep as something of a gamble, but this has the advantage that if a shark is hooked on another line, you can leave the distant deep one out where it won't tangle and keep fishing. If you put your baits all at the same depth and huddle them close together you must reel in the lines that are free as soon as possible, otherwise a tangle could lose the angler his fish. Try to conduct yourselves like sportsmen rather than greedy individuals who couldn't care less about your fellow anglers. I have given more shark runs away that I care to remember. After you have had a few, why not let your friends in on the excitement? Especially if it is their first shark.

There is absolutely no way of knowing what fish is going to be on the end of your line, and if you give a fish strike away, you are playing into the hands of the gods, who then dish out all the decent fish. Only ten days before starting this book, on a trip to Inisbofin Island off the west coast of Galway, Ireland, I gave away two good fish. Like so many times before, the first shark of the day came to my rod, after I decided the wind and tidal conditions dictated deep-set baits. It worked and I tagged and released a nice 55-lb blue. Seconds later my other rod screamed out, so thinking it was another mediocre fish I gave my rod to my friend Adrian Hutchins. He was on his first shark trip for about three years and badly wanted to pull on a bent rod. After a tremendous struggle on a 30-lb rod he boated his biggest ever shark, a blue of 80 lb! I had given away a good fish. Next day I decided on a really deep bait, and tied three ounces of lead inside a hooked mackerel to keep it down in the rough water. A run came, only a mile offshore, and I gave the run to my wife Hilary, realising that there was every possibility that so close to rocky shores it could be a porbeagle. She struck, was harnessed up on the bucking 30-lb Fenwick rod, and dropped the Aftco butt into the Sampo butt pad. In a rough sea she did a good job on the fish, which turned out to be

In it comes! Graeme wires a big 90 lb Blue aboard for his wife, Hilary, who hooked the shark aboard the *Goldseeker* from Inisbofin Island using just 30 lb tackle. You can see the serrated teeth on this shark, which was unhooked and returned alive. It was the first shark landed by a woman from Inisbofin.

Kite fishing is something new to British anglers but the author has used this technique to capture Hammerheads off the Florida Keys of up to 160 lb. It allows up to two extra lines to be run on the downwind side of the boat, out of harm's way, and where it doesn't tangle with other lines.

There is one vital factor to a good day's fishing. If the rubby trail is broken, you lose the trail altogether so at least make sure someone is shaking the bags every five minutes. Better still, bring the bags aboard and give them a good stamping. This releases more oil.

With fresh mackerel, the only way to break them down into a fine mix is by mincing. You can buy old mincers at car boot sales for about 50p. Try to get one with a big 'neck' and wide holes to cut quickly. Wash out and change if clogged with skin.

The author's rig for deep water Porbeagles. A whole 2 lb Pollock is split so that the entrails hang out, then a mesh bag the size of a large orange is filled with rubby and tied close to the hook. This gets a smell down to deep water where surface rubby cannot reach. This is excellent for running out a couple of baits when fishing rough ground at anchor while going after other species.

Here's a novel idea from Mike Benwell, the skipper of *Sportfisher 1*, who saw Graeme take Gambian sharks of 300 and 355 lb on an exploratory trip on his boat. Mike made up this baitdropper from old drainpipe to get the rubby dubby down on the bottom quickly instead of being whisked away on the tide. It could be incorporated in British sharking at anchor.

The continual overfishing of prime food sources like the mackerel is illustrated by this picture of 20 odd tons of mackerel being unloaded from just one trawler at Killybegs harbour. No doubt the species will have to near extinction before it becomes protected. Deprived of their main food chain baitfish we are probably looking at fewer numbers of shark – despite our own conservation efforts.

Left: The small mouth of this Thresher of 130 lb can be seen. Never be afraid to use a Mustad Seamaster in the 6/0 range for small livebaits when Thresher fishing.

Facing: 'A man after my own heart!' proclaimed Graeme after a session with Capt. Luis Laje in the Azores. They were after Mako, so Luis simply obtained more rubby by gutting one of the sharks Graeme had landed, extracting the liver and 'stamping' it down into a pulp. They caught another Mako using the mixture but when doing it yourself, make sure that the Mako's liver you are extracting is *very* dead – and that you have long wellies on!

Below: Taking the backbone out of mackerel hookbaits makes them softer to a finicky shark that may have eaten too much previously or may even have consumed too much rubby. Use only small mesh bags and don't allow large chunks of fish to be thrown in the water. You want to attract the sharks, not feed them!

Above: A fine Whitetip shark, hooked by the author, surges near the boat.

Facing above: Sharks on light gear can be fun. Here the author puts the max on a near 100 lb shark using just a 20 lb line. A Shimano TLD reel with its silky smooth drag and a 12 lb class Fenwick Woodstream rod blank meant Graeme was well within the safety limits.

Facing below: A 'ton-up' Thresher glides past the boat prior to gaffing. Note the big pectoral fins to give it good turning speed.

A superb close-up of a large Thresher showing clearly the small mouth of this species. Threshers of up to 400 lb or more are believed to swim near British shores.

The author has had many other species 'hit' by sharks while he has played them. Just look at the incredible devastation to this 130 lb Yellowfin tuna after it was hit by a pack of Whitetip sharks. Looking at the remains, it is evident that some sharks took 15 lb of meat in one bite!

Above: The grim expression says it all. Hilary Pullen fights a shark in a force 6 gale while Adrian Hutchins looks on waiting for the wire trace to show.

Facing: The author became the first angler to take a shark from the previously unfished Inisbofin Island on Ireland's rugged West Coast. The fish was released.

Left: The coloured tags used by anglers when releasing sharks. Recaptured sharks have revealed amazing statistics on distances travelled.

Graeme and skipper George Burgum prepare to release a big Blue landed by Graeme on light tackle. The fish bears an Inland Fisheries Trust (now CFB) tag and its recapture may reveal important statistics about the species's growth rate and migration pattern.

just under the Irish specimen weight, and kicked the scales down to 96 lb, a fair old blue on 30-lb line! I remember giving another angler from Dorking a strike out in the Azores. There had been a mix-up over who should be using my curved butt 50 trolling rod, and the fish I landed subsequently was a fine Atlantic blue marlin of 304 lb. I am still adamant that I was in the right, as I have never taken another angler's rod, or even been given a strike by an English shark or marlin angler, but as a gentleman I thought the best way to resolve the situation and avoid a session of the sulks was to give my own strike away, whatever it was. I ran the risk of giving away a record-busting marlin of course, but there it was, I had made the offer, and it was accepted. Next day the strike came, and the angler concerned boated a massive big eye tuna of 175 lb! Of course such mix-ups are bound to fuel the jealous gossips, even friends on the same boat, who instantly side against you, despite your doing the 'correct' thing. It is better to let a novice have a fish if you yourself are an experienced angler.

One time I even gave a strike to our skipper. Ted Legge, the Gosport shark skipper, was driving a boat on Faial island in the Azores, and although he had boated a few fish, luck had eluded him. Then I arrived with a party of English anglers and we started fishing in earnest with some of my modern lures. One day we had phenomenal luck, sharing the fish round so everybody on the boat got one. As we ran for home with four huge marlin aboard I sat thinking about poor old Ted up on the bridge. That he was not just an enthusiastic skipper I knew, for his idea of a holiday from commercial and charter boat sharking was . . . to go fishing! Although delighted with our catch I thought he must be heartbroken not to be one of the anglers himself. He wouldn't get anything out of the other anglers on the boat, so I tackled each one individually about giving Ted the next strike, if of course it ever came. I could see from their faces that at first they weren't in favour, but eventually they agreed, and I spoke with Brenda, Ted's wife who was sitting on a side seat with her feet on a pile of marlin to 762 lb. Ted obviously had his pride, and I feared that he might not take the strike, and come down from the flying bridge. I explained to Brenda that she had to back me up in getting Ted to take it, and to add to the excitement, I decided not to tell him until the fish was hooked up. It's a hard man who refuses a fish that's screaming out line! As luck would have it, the stinger line twanged and a marlin crashed into a lure and roared away. Immediately Ted gunned the engines to help set the hooks, and I screamed at him above the engine noise that it was his strike. For a second or two he hesitated, we shouted at each other, and then he was shinning down the ladder to take the rod. He was like a kid in a sweetshop with a licence to eat anything. With me to operate the boat controls the gears got crunched more than once, but we took that fish, Ted's biggest Atlantic blue at the time . . . and 305 lb! It's not often you return to port with everyone aboard a gameboat having caught a marlin—including the skipper! A present from me Ted, I'm just glad it wasn't 600-plus!

When you get the situation I've described when the wind is quartering the tide, careful observation of the trail direction will ensure you locate your bait in the correct position. Most anglers think that the direction they see the pilchard oil slick taking on the surface is the direction the trail is going. Yet in putting out their distant deep baits they may well have one that is hanging outside the slick altogether. What happens in reality is this. The bags are tied to the side of the boat, so they get a continual dunking in the water caused by the rocking of the boat, which allows an even distribution of the fish particles. These particles sink, while the oil floats to the surface. Anything that floats on the surface is at the mercy of the wind, so the oil slick follows the directional bearing of the wind. The particles which release this oil trail are also what will attract any shark, and these are affected by the tide, not the wind. Again it will fluctuate throughout a day's drifting, as the tide ebbs, floods or becomes slack water. The easiest way to gauge which way the tidal stream is taking the sub surface fish particles is to drop down a free bottom line with about three or four ounces of lead on it. If depth allows let it hit the bottom; you may then be surprised to see this line angled off towards either the bow or the stern. That is the direction of the trail. Your baits should be set correspondingly, and probably brought in closer.

A tip to save you getting a line cut off by a taking shark, is to run out the deepest and therefore farthest bait first. Then run out and set

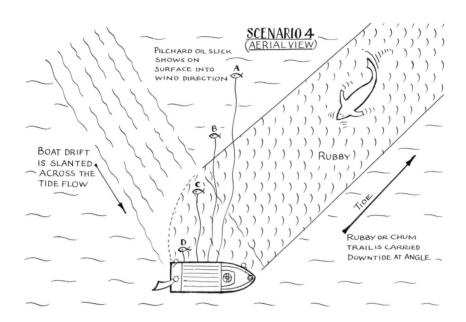

the next closest, the next and so on. If you get a shark on and have to bring in the other lines, try to maintain a little decorum and run that distant bait out first again. Of course everyone wants to get their lines back in the water quickly, but what is the point of being greedy, when you may get cut off through running the steel trace of one line across the mono of another? I've seen it happen many times, which is why I now seldom share a boat with strangers, sticking to friends who know the procedure to follow. The most lines I have organised was eight. That was on a press trip to Ireland where of course everyone wanted to have a shark line in the water. I was allocated the job of sorting it all out, and I am pleased to say that the day in question was a success with every single angler getting a blue shark. We had a couple of tangles, but nothing serious, and I even managed a couple of 80 pounders myself in between setting other people's lines!

I have already mentioned the subject of floats, but there is another tip that few realise can have an effect on your catch rate. As I have mentioned, the tidal flow can actually be slanting off at a different angle to that indicated by the surface oil and you need to adjust bait settings accordingly. If you are using a balloon, and most sharkers do, you will not have noticed that, like the surface slick of oil, it is affected by the wind, which can affect its position in the sub surface slick. Materials like cork though will bob under more often and being less susceptible to wind hang in the tidal flow better. For this reason I carry floats made of several materials, but invariably end up using a cork float in a wind-across-tide situation. One of the best old lines I first used was 55-lb Searanger which was a braided terylene and floated through the waves. It was great to be able to see this tighten when a shark was fiddling with the bait, but as it floated it tended to be bowed by any wind. Coupled to a balloon you could be yards outside the slick on a fresh wind. For that reason I use exclusively monofilament, which sinks, and is pulled by the tide better.

Anchoring

While drifting is surely the most popular method of shark fishing in use in British and European waters, it is worth noting that an anchored boat has the advantage of covering no bottom ground, which a boat pushed by the wind would do. It also eliminates many of the wind-across-tide situations that demand careful placing of baits to optimise results. Anchoring is best for inshore or localised shark species, like porbeagles in British waters, or the reef sharks in tropical waters. Abroad of course, where you have a sharp drop-off from shallow inshore reef water to deep blue water of several hundred metres, then you have the additional chance of pulling up a big ocean-roaming shark, like a tiger, bull, hammerhead or sand shark.

The best method for sharking over an area of rock is not to anchor right on top of that rock, but first to find the greatest run of tidal flow in one direction, i.e. the full time of the ebb or the flood. Then position your boat about 300 yards uptide from the rock, allowing for any wind, which allows your rubby slick to sink and drift over the rock, pulling off any predators that may be feeding there. If you anchor right on top of the rock, by the time your rubby slick has sunk to the shark's depth it will be miles away. It is better to take time positioning the boat for the period of tidal flow that will push the rubby slick onto the rock. Make sure the anchor is fitted with a quick-release rope, and buoy for collecting later. If you hit a big shark, you want to get after him straight away to get some line on the reel, and if you stay at anchor you run the risk of the fish doubling back and wrapping the line around the anchor rope.

This procedure is best when using deadbaits, and as you will have a much narrower area of distribution, namely off the stern, there should be a limit to the number of rods. I would advise staggering two baits under a float, setting one rod three-quarters of the water depth off the rock, and running it some way back, perhaps a hundred yards. The other I would set at a quarter of the water depth and about forty yards back. These can be propped in each corner of the stern. I would then fit one shark trace/bait up on a running leger with a giant 12-inch clement's boom fashioned from a wire coathanger, and attach a pound or so of lead to drop it to the bottom. When you hit bottom, wind up a few times to keep it from snagging. Finally keep a fourth rod in reserve, ready to be baited up and dropped back to any shark that appears near the boat and has missed the baits. I would use sand mixed in with the mashed fish, which helps to take the mixture down quickly, and can even be squeezed into balls and dropped over to sink to greater depths.

Another thing to remember when you fish directly over an area of reef or rock is that the rubby trail will have little effect on the sharks. They are living there specifically because the concentration of other fish is high, so they rarely need stimulating to feed. This applies to the porbeagle in colder waters as much as it does to tigers, bulls and hammerheads in the tropics. What they do like is a nice fresh live or deadbait, preferably oozing a bit of blood as a locator. I have found that smearing a bit of pilchard oil onto a livebait enhances its appeal, and can be added in seconds. Livebaiting is one of the best ways to take sharks, and I would say that our own porbeagle, being an eater of pelagic fish, will respond better to a well-presented livebait than to a deadbait. Certainly when fishing the tropics, a bleeding live fish acts on both the olfactory sense of a shark and the ampullae of Lorenzeni which they use to detect electrical impulses.

Livebaiting is also successful when drifting, but more so with porbeagle and mako than blue. One of the best ways is to hook a mackerel lightly through the dorsal fin, either in front or behind, and simply drop it over the side without a float. You can fish it with a free spool and ratchet on, or providing you have some sort of rod holder, leave the reel on strike drag. This is a good method for both thresher and porbeagle when the rubby trail is going straight down underneath the boat. I feel a great many fish are lost because anglers fail to realise just how close to the boat some sharks will come. One of the best ways to hook a mackerel for livebait quickly is by taking the hook in through the top of the lip and out through a nostril vent. This way, when they get tired, they will be dragged by the drifting boat to allow water to flow over the gills and keep them fresh. But by far the best way to keep a livebait fresh and pumping away all day is by bridle-rigging through the front of the eye sockets. Primarily used as a means of slow trolling big tuna livebaits for marlin, it can be used by European shark anglers, or indeed anywhere in the world where sharks are to be caught. Only recently I bridle-rigged pollock up to 5 lb while porbeagle fishing off Mizen Head in south-west Ireland and the skipper was amazed to see how fit the pollock were. The secret with pollock, which are a primary food of the porbeagle, is to wind them up very slowly when catching them for bait. They tend to blow up their air bladder when dragged through the depths too quickly, and do not live long under such conditions. If you speed-wind them to the surface, they not only don't live long, but they float as well! Then they are only good for a specimen black-backed gull!

Bridle-rigging is a bit fiddly, and must be done quickly and efficiently if the livebait is to stay alive properly. I have done a lot of livebaiting for marlin and sharks, and have managed to unhook, bridle-rig, and put a pollock in the water in just 17 seconds. Obviously the quicker and more efficiently you work the better, especially with mackerel which are very difficult to keep alive even in an aerated live well. You can sometimes make do with a large freshwater keepnet, tying it at the side and taking a fresh bait whenever you need one. A bait rigged properly allows the hook to be folded over when the bait is taken head first, and it will be pointing in the right direction when you strike.

Deep Dropping

While drifting is the best method for all round sharking, and anchoring the best for specific species, there is another method known as 'deep dropping'. This consists of firing a bait down into a very deep area where sharks are thought to be present. It may be an area of rough ground or a wreck, but it is generally water so deep that rubby dubby will not get down in the precise area. I have used it many times in tropical waters, but have never seen anyone use it in Europe. A big bait, either a whole tuna fish or a side of amberjack is rigged on double shark hooks. To the bend of the hook is tied a piece of 30-lb dacron line, and about ten feet along that is tied a weight—something expendable like a rock, a paving slab or a piece of scrap iron. This is to get the bait down quickly, and to combat any tidal or ocean currents that may act on line and bait, swinging them towards the surface. You need to get the bait down, and to keep it there. When a shark hits the bait and starts to snap and chew, he will sever the piece of dacron thus allowing the weight to fall free. You can then hook the shark unhindered. It is an excellent method, although it may appear crude at first. It enables you to fish areas of the ocean where the biggest sharks often swim.

A method used by a Plymouth skipper many years ago was to motor out to deep water and using his Decca Navigator for precise location, drop five-gallon drums of mashed fish guts over the side. The drums had been punctured and weighted with rocks to take them as straight down as possible. He could do this on the way out to deep-water wrecks, and with the Decca co-ordinates recorded, he could take a day out to fish for sharks every so often, knowing where they would be. The species he caught most were porbeagles, which shows that they will go down to the bottom, even in forty fathoms of water, and can be taken on a bait fished on a flowing trace. This skipper took blues like this, and was broken up a couple of times by bigger sharks.

Off the port of Weymouth another group of anglers were working along similar lines. They too took average-sized porbeagles, not drifting on the surface, but on bottom baits fished over rough ground. They also took some huge conger as well as the sharks. Only

Go Fishing for Shark

Previous skipper of the *Security*, Brian Furphy has the measure of this fish which he has shortened up on the leader. Small sharks of up to 70 lb can be dragged aboard if the hookhold is good. Anything larger will need jaw gaffing to bring aboard.

recently the port of Poole in Dorset has seen some very big porbeagle sharks taken by a group of anglers who believe that they have located a new school of sharks that work east up to the Isle of Wight grounds. When the Island skippers lose them, the lads of Poole start catching. They believe they are the same fish that work back to the west, staying off Poole Bay to feed on the mackerel shoals that hole up there. They have taken fish over 200 lb, and twice they have had enormous sharks around the boat. I received a phone call one evening asking me to advise them on lures for catching what they thought were huge mako sharks. These fish were in excess of 500 lb. I advised trolling, as these big makos had ignored both live and deadbaits fished in the strongest part of the rubby trail.

Trolling

Trolling with either livebaits, deadbaits or lures is yet another way to take sharks in both temperate and tropical waters. No smell trail is required, but certain lures seem to work better than others. Big flashing spoons work well at lower speeds, and can be rigged up with three feet of 'chewin' wire, crimped by a swivel to ten feet of heavy-duty monofilament to avoid the rough hide of the shark chafing through the line. The largest size of the American 'pet' spoons is ideal for slow speeds. Yozuri also manufacture a rubber-winged flying fish that is weighted by a lead chin strap. Primarily used for fishing giant bluefin tuna they are also good for attracting sharks as the tail-throbbing action and wiggle send out tremendous vibrations that the sharks home in on.

Just six months ago I was fishing the CMC-sponsored fishing tournament off Watamu in Kenya, and was up in the flying bridge tower of 'Muff' Becker's gameboat the *El Dorado*. I had already missed a hook-up on a 250-lb blue marlin way out deep on one of Ed Murray's Boston mackerel artificials. From the flying bridge I could look back down the sun and see through the water better. Suddenly a grey shape appeared behind the lure, tracking it from only six feet away. It was a huge shark, a grey shape with a long pointed snout, and I can only think it was a massive mako. However, we had no bait aboard, and after tracking us for several minutes the shark departed.

The Yozuri rubber flying fish comes in two sizes and has a pair of enlarged plastic pectoral fins that can be bent out to change the action. I think the smaller size would be good for European sharks, and to that end I have now rigged mine on wire. Some species of shark, especially the mako, have the ability to catch a standard trolled marlin lure. They are hard plastic and tend to run better when trolled at faster speeds from 7 knots upwards. I have now had a couple of mako myself on a marlin lure, and seen a couple more. For European fishing, however, I feel the slower speeds at which the Yozuri flying fish and pet spoons are trolled would be better suited to both our colder water and the wallet of the boat skipper. It's better by far to slow troll inshore areas for porbeagle or mako using either a rigged livebait or deadbait. Slow trolling is $1^1/2$ to 2 knots, which is about right to keep the baits swimming behind the boat—too slow and they can double over each other and tangle, too fast and they break up or die. In the tropics it is standard procedure to slow troll tuna livebaits for sharks or marlin, using the bridle-rig described above. This is done using outriggers or downriggers. The outriggers space the lines apart, and a livebait can be checked by holding the pulley rope to the outrigger clip across your thumb and index finger. You should be able to feel the tuna bait thrumming away on the end. If you can't it's either died naturally, or has been taken by a smaller shark. When using baits on the downrigger it is possible to detect these livebait vibrations but to a lesser degree. Therefore it may be necessary to check the bait every hour or so, taking care not to damage it. It's better to run the downrigger clip very light so the slightest pull will release it. A drop-back, or belly of line is also allowed to enable a taking fish to feel no resistance, the reel having been put on the lightest drag possible, with the audible check engaged to prevent an overrun.

When trolling European and British waters it is not always possible to find livebait over the ground where you think the sharks are. When you can't use livebait follow the same procedure as for bridle-rigging a livebait, but use a fresh dead one. From a British boat, which will have no outriggers, you can only troll a pair of livebaits, fitting one rod to each corner of the boat. You can make a portable rod holder from a 24-inch length of heavy-duty plastic piping, tying it to the gunwales.

Of all the British sharks to respond to trolling, the porbeagle is best. They like a moving bait, and working from a moving bait you are safe to work close inshore to rocks and cliffs that you couldn't otherwise reach. I would advise setting only a very light drag with an audible check as you want the shark to take and turn the bait before striking. Clear the other rod out of the way as soon as you get a strike. A method worth employing when running two rods like this is to rig a 'daisy chain' of other mackerel up the line, tying them at intervals of two feet using 20-lb dacron. Make sure you sew their mouths shut. This crashing, splashing action will have more chance of bringing up a marauding shark from the depths, and should he snatch one of the baits held on by dacron it will still leave him free to come back for another. He will take the last bait in the chain, and of course this is the one with the hook in it. I would advise half-hitching no more than five other small mackerel on the line above the hookbait. This method of course is for use only with a deadbait and not a livebait.

Kite Fishing

This is probably the most exciting, principally because it is the newest as far as European sharking goes. As far as I am aware I am the first British angler to run six shark lines, with two of them on the downwind side of a drifting boat. If you think about it for a minute, common sense will tell you that any bait you put in the water on this side will drag back up underneath the hull, and if you hook a fish you will only lose it. However, I have been running four shark lines in the rubby drift in the slick, as per normal, but I have run a double-rigger kite line with baits supended on the downwind side of the hull!

I developed this idea when I found over the years that a number of sharks suddenly appeared at the back or downwind beam of the boat, apparently having swum up the rubby slick and past my waiting baits. Occasionally I picked up fish with bait on a rod hanging over the side by the rubby sack. Some of those sharks, especially those swimming into a strong tide, would just keep on swimming after losing the smell trail, and simply swim on past the boat.

With the wind blowing the boat along, I could run a kite line out behind on the downwind side, and by attaching two Aftco roller troller outrigger clips, run another two lines with baits on an intercept course outside the rubby trail. I had taken sharks before on a kite, out of Miami where I fished with Bouncer Smith in his centre console gameboat. He showed me how to perfect kite fishing for sharks on the open ocean, and my two largest hammerheads of that trip both came on a proper fishing kite. The method is centuries old, but was adapted for sailfish in the Florida Keys about thirty or forty years ago. My hammerhead sharks weighed 140 lb and 160 lb, which taken with such an unusual method and on only 30-lb tackle set me thinking. If all British and Irish shark skippers ran at least one kite line, I wonder how many 'bonus' sharks could they too pick up?

Go Fishing for Shark

KITE FISHING

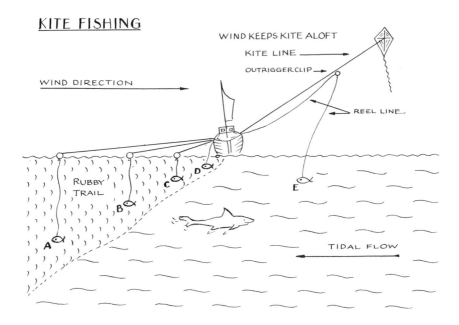

The beauty of this method is that for our European standard drifting methods you need a good breeze anyway, so flying a kite depends only on the type you wish to use. If you hook a fish on the usual side of the boat, you can still leave the kite lines in the water as the line runs from rod top to outrigger roller clip then straight down into the sea. There is no loose line lying on the surface, so those rods can stay out all day. With the Aftco roller trollers set at different spacings up your kite line you can adjust the depth at which those baits are fishing, and have no need even to move the rod or attach a float. When a shark takes, the outrigger roller clip pops open, and you are attached to him without him knowing a thing!

I can't think why nobody in British sharking circles has ever used this technique before, as it can also be adapted for trolling or skipping a bait along the surface behind the boat. This way all line is kept off the water, and the boat can be speeded up or slowed down to suit wind conditions. This is a method that I am sure more anglers will now want to try, and I am sure it will bring them success. Even if you fail to get a shark run from those kite rods on your first trip, it can be amusing to play with the kite! Using a kite may also be the only real way to get at some of the porbeagle sharks to make that shore-caught record, and I have every intention of giving Inisbofin Island a good try, from the North Bay where I once lost a shark from the shore.

Shore and Shallow Water Fishing

In warmer climes there is every chance of taking a shark from both shallow water, and the shore. I have done both myself, and can attest to the fact that it is some of the most exciting shark sport available. This is due mainly to its visual aspect and the fact that when out wading you are stalking your quarry in exciting and nerve-racking fashion. You also have no sanctuary as you do with a boat, and while there is little chance of being attacked by a 'skinny water shark', I wouldn't advise the angler to go wading in an area he has groundbaited with mashed fish!

There are three methods in water of four feet or less. You can fish from a small skiff, go wading across a bonefish flat, or simply fish from the shore. The way to take a shark on light tackle visually is either to go looking for one, or fish so that they come to you. If there are plenty of small sharks about on the shallows you fish, sharks like bonnetheads, nurse or blacktips, then I would say go wading for them. That way you can cover a lot of ground and cast to each fish individually.

The best baits are freshly killed pinfish or grunts, or better still half a balao. No weight is required, but you will need a good strong 3/0 hook and a couple of feet of wire. To this you can attach a stronger length of 50-lb monofilament as a rubbing leader, about another six feet or so. This prevents them rolling up and chafing your main line with their rough hide. When you make a cast don't throw too near the fish or it will take fright. Even sharks are nervous when they have eighteen inches of water covering their backs!

Most flats will have a tidal flow across them, so working on the principle that most sharks on the flats will be working their way into the tide, try to throw the bait well ahead, and uptide of them. Invariably they will pick up the scent, but a tip I have used successfully in the Florida Keys is to rub pilchard oil on the bait before casting. Then I deliberately cast beyond the path of the fish, wind back slowly and let the bait settle on the bottom as near as I can get to where the fish will pass. If he looks like missing the bait he can pick up that oily smell, and will switch round to home in on the bait. It is a simple trick, but you'll be surprised how many times I've seen it work. Another bait that works well is a hookload of shrimps. They must give off a good smell because I've seen many small bonnetheads literally whip round to gobble them up!

Another way to catch a shark from the shallows is to set out your stall, anchor your skiff either right on the flat or at the edge of the channel, and put over a bag of minced chum. The tide will carry it away, and it shouldn't be too long before you pick out the odd shape weaving its way towards you in the distance as it tries to locate the source of that delicious smell. Some people like to cast out a couple of baits in the chum trail and wait, lying in the boat with a can of Budweiser and generally taking things easy. But I keep my baits in the boat until the shark is close enough to cast to, because small pinfish and grunts will often pick your hook clean while you doze in the sun. When the sharks are bumping the boat you suddenly wake up and don't have a bait in the water! The vigilant angler generally catches the most, besides which it is fascinating to watch a shark weave its way towards the smell.

Don't be surprised to find other species also taking an avid interest in the chum lane. I've had stingrays to 50 lb hooked up on spinning rods baited with shrimps, seen bonefish scouring the bottom when the only bait I've had in the boat was a whole balao, and had nurse sharks bumbling about trying for ten minutes to locate a fish bait only two feet from them. Barracuda also move into chum slicks, presumably attracted by the activities of the smaller fish. The largest I've taken like this weighed 21 lb. It is even possible, if you can't get hold of any fresh 'meat' in the shape of frozen chum, to attract fish with a mixture of bread, bran and pilchard oil. This brings in the small fish which you then catch on very small hooks and fine lines, cutting them up and throwing them into an area downtide. Sharks need very little scent to follow up and in shallow depths a weaker smell can travel further because the volume of water is less.

British Species

Blue Shark

This species is the most prolific shark in UK waters, and it is therefore the most sought after. Local commercial fishermen working the long lines on the offshore reefs have obviously known that blue sharks were present in our home waters for years, but it was not until the Shark Angling Club of Great Britain was formed in the spring of 1953 that the sport really became popular. At that time, to apply for membership you had to be proposed and seconded by an existing member, and produce proof of capture of a shark weighing over 75 lb. To give an idea of numbers, in 1953 360 sharks were weighed in by members, 340 of them at Looe in Cornwall, and membership was 48. In 1956, 1972 sharks were caught and membership was 224. Over the next fifteen years the numbers of blue shark recorded rose to over 2000, but by then they were being killed in such large numbers that a decline inevitably took place.

With the decline in shark numbers came a decline in interest, and now Looe, once a thriving centre for tourist shark anglers, shows few signs of its former glory. I have known 25 boats to set sail for the blue shark grounds from this port alone, but you would be pushed to find half a dozen now, and that in mid-season.

Go Fishing for Shark

We have mostly female blue sharks around our British coastline, while the United States East Coast has a high percentage of males. The male fish distinguish themselves by claspers, as seen in the lower of the two fish.

While overkill by anglers is the main reason for the decline, I am of the opinion that two other factors are present. At around the same time as the shark decline, came the discovery by our commercial fishermen of the overwintering grounds of our main pelagic food fish, the mackerel. Spawning grounds draw enormous numbers of any fish, and in consequence untold damage was done by commercial fishermen of all countries interested in making a fast buck. There were even stories of nets so full of mackerel that they couldn't be lifted from the water, even by hydraulics. The nets were cut away, and the tons of dead fish sank to the bottom. Anglers all round Britain suddenly found that all fishing was now difficult as the mackerel was nearing localised extinction.

The other factor in the decline in interest is cost. Suddenly fuel prices soared and the cost of a day's charter rose considerably. Tourists gave up the idea of trying to catch a shark while on holiday, so there were fewer boats fishing for sharks anyway.

British Species

In the last couple of years, there have been restrictions on the number of mackerel the commercials can catch. Hopefully this is having a reviving effect on the fish stocks, for many anglers now find they can feather up enough bait for a session or two. With the increase in baitfish comes the return of the blue, and this past season has been one of the best ever for this species, with a high average weight per fish.

Anglers don't kill every fish they catch. While it's fine to keep the odd one for a picture or crab pot bait, there is far more to be gained by adopting the tag and release programme. Not only does the fish have a chance of survival, but its recapture can give essential information to research groups.

For blue sharks it is essential to use a couple of bags of rubby dubby. This method originated in the Cornish port of Polperro, where locals used to hang a bag of fish heads and guts over the side when they were handlining for large mackerel. In the United States it is known as chum, and may consist of finely minced fish, or simply chunks cut up into cubes and tossed overboard. It was but a short step from Polperro to Looe, and subsequently the shark anglers tried this method, with a plentiful supply of pilchard heads and guts thrown out by the local canning factory. The pilchard has a very high oil content, and while the canning factory has long since closed I still advocate the use of pilchard oil in the rubby mix.

In that early era members of the Club thought the period from 1 pm to 5 pm was the best for taking blues. The reason for this is simply that when drifting, it usually takes that long to get a good trail going. Once you have a substantial slick I think it is only a matter of an hour or so for the sharks to catch up with the drifting boat and find your baits. Actual time has no relevance.

While an average blue shark today may weigh 40 or 50 lb, its weight dropped to nearer 25–30 lb during the peak of its decline. The current British record stands at just over 200 lb and must be virtually unbeatable now, but with sharking you never really know what size has taken the bait. The largest I can find a trace of in British waters came off the port of Polperro just after the Second World War. It was landed on a handline and weighed 350 lb! There is an account of another at 263 lb being taken off Aberdovey in Wales by a herring

65

Go Fishing for Shark

A formidable array of teeth shown by a blue shark. This triangular shape has a serrated edge to each tooth and is effective for cutting. Ragged teeth with no serrations, like Porbeagle and Mako, are designed more for tearing, and consequently stronger jaw muscles are present.

drifter. On the world scene, for rod and line catches, the International Game Fishing Association (IGFA) have a massive 437 lb blue recorded, taken by an angler using just 30 lb line in New South Wales, Australia. We are never likely to see such a fish in British waters, but the Azores archipelago to the west of Madeira has had blues over 400 lb recorded. Doubtless this species will grow to more than 700 lb, especially the ocean wanderers.

These larger-than-average specimens were once referred to as blue whalers, from their habits of following in the wake of the old whaling ships, often tearing at the whale carcases being dragged behind. They are unpredictable in warmer tropical waters and have been linked to attacks on sailors of ships sunk during the Second World War. While a blue doesn't have the fighting power of the mako or porbeagle it does have a beauty in the water that is lovely to see. A magnificent cobalt blue, with white underbelly and long pointed snout are the first things you notice when you spot a blue at the side of the boat.

They have a tendency to 'roll up' during the fight, a point which enables them to wrap all of the steel leader around their body and rub through your main line. For that reason it is best to incorporate a double line of ten feet or so, as a safety factor. Only two weeks ago a friend, Adrian Hutchins landed an 80-lb blue from Ireland and found that it had wrapped up and rolled itself into the double line, one length of which was severed. Had he been using a single line he would have lost the fish.

Blues are not too particular about bait presentation. While the freshest bait is always best, I have taken them to just under 200 lb in the Azores on pieces of tuna and mako shark intestine all carefully wrapped round a double-hook rig. I don't know who was more surprised when we hooked up, the shark or me! I've also caught them on pollock and whiting when bait stocks have run out and the best method I have found is to fish a split tail mackerel bait, a bait I once popularised for tope and monkfish, but which has now been christened by somebody as the 'flapper'. I don't feel it's the movement that attracts the shark, but more the juices that this bait releases.

The blue is a deep-water shark, seldom venturing in depths less than twenty fathoms, more often working the forty-fathom line. For

Go Fishing for Shark

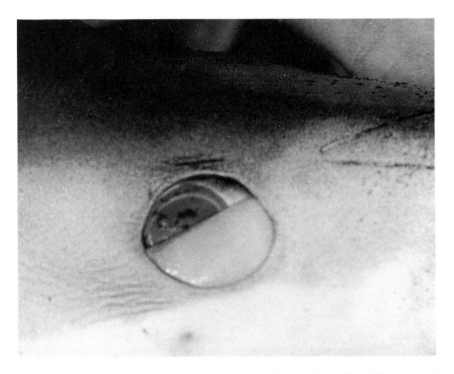

The shark has a fold of skin which it slides over its eye when attacking a fish. This protects it against damage.

most of the British coastline this means a good run offshore, but I have taken them within a mile from shore on the Isles of Scilly and at Inisbofin Island off County Galway in Ireland. This latter venue gave me 53 fathoms just a mile and half from shore, so if you want some exploratory sharking in an area that screams big shark, you could do worse than try there in August and September. Aptly enough there is another island that we use as a landmark when fishing from Inisbofin—it's called *Inishark!* There simply has to be some good shark there!

I would put the blue shark down as the most obliging species likely to be encountered around the British coastline, primarily following the North Atlantic Drift which is the final finger of the Gulf Stream, that warm-water artery that comes up along the eastern seaboard of

British Species

the United States. He seems to like to feed in depths of forty fathoms or more over clean sand, but don't let that deter you from trying an area of rock offshore, or comparatively close to shore where the depth is more than twenty fathoms. In tropical waters they seldom visit inshore shallow areas of water, but will certainly run the edge of reef lines where there is a drop-off into deep blue water. Fished on light tackle they are a worthy adversary, and are rated by the IGFA as a game shark. While some malign its fighting qualities it is generally because they have them on only 80-lb and 130-lb test tackle. My advice is to use nothing more than 30-lb test—20-lb is adequate and even 12-lb will give you a good scrapping fish. While I have eaten some of the tail section, which tastes somewhat like pork, there is no real reason to kill them, short of recording a personal best or a record, so why not put them back? Although it is slightly hazardous, you can still get photographs in the boat, and you can use a weight-for-length table to give you some idea of its weight.

Porbeagle

This is a short, stubby, porky little fish that is far more prolific than was previously thought, and gives the angler a good fight for his money. They feed almost entirely on mackerel and pollock, working very close to shore in rocky areas. The main reason I think more of them are being caught now, apart from a change in fashion, is that the food fish chain has changed. Ten years ago we saw a massive decline in the numbers of mackerel, as I have explained above. This left a gap in the chain that was filled by the coalfish. There have never been so many small 1—2 lb coalfish about as there are now, and they appear to have spread a long way south from the colder waters where in theory they should be. The porbeagles feed heavily on them, and so anglers are finding more to catch.

This species of shark can be caught in water only thirty feet deep, right up against the most jagged rocks and cliffs, a point which makes them the only species of shark in British waters that is really a viable proposition for taking from the shore. This has been done before of course, but only by one man. Jack Shine from Ireland fished from a mark known as Green Island. This is at the mouth of Liscannor Bay,

69

some five miles from the resort of Lahinch. It is in fact joined to the mainland by rocks and can only technically be called an island during the top three hours of the tide when these rocks are covered. Jack located the porbeagles quite innocently while spinning with goat's hair flies for mackerel. He had the lot taken by a huge fish which broke the line. He cast out again wth tope tackle and hooked a porbeagle immediately, a fish around 120 lb, but lost that too. He became determined to take the first ever shark from the shore and so rigged up with adequate tackle and persevered. His first success came with the capture of a 77-lb porbeagle. He took two more later—75 lb and 91 lb. He fished the following year, 1963 to take fish of 106 lb, 130 lb, 90 lb, 101 lb and 138 lb, an incredible catch that has never been equalled by any other angler. As one who has taken more than a few sharks I have the greatest respect for Jack Shine, who with the minimum of tackle and the maximum patience achieved a feat that has never been repeated. Not one shark has been landed from the shore by an angler for over 25 years, although I did lose one at Insbofin Island to the same method as Jack when he first discovered them, spinning for mackerel and pollock.

It appeared that the many shark boats of the early years were steaming out *over* some of the best shark grounds and shark anglers began to try the inshore rock marks off north Cornwall and Devon. Success was immediate, mostly from marks between Hartland Point, west to Tintagel. The world record listings took a hammering with some huge fish caught. The main concern of many serious anglers was that too many sharks were being killed. Porbeagles make money on the fish market and some skippers not only charged a high price for a day's charter, but sold the fish caught, often for more than the cost of the charter. While some still fish there, many dedicated anglers will no longer fish this area because of the greed of some skippers in killing the sharks. These range from obese pregnant females that are used to claim world records, right down to immature fifty-pounders, that anybody can see, should not be extracted in numbers. One would think they would have learned the lesson of the destruction of the south Cornwall blue shark fishery, but apparently not, the fast buck still reigns supreme.

Something like eight world records are held by British anglers, indicative that we probably have the best porbeagle shark fishing in the world. Several fish of 400 lb and more have been taken from an area of rock running out from the cliffs known as Crackinton Haven. The 80-lb men's world record is held by Derek Runnals with a fish of 458 lblb, caught on 15 May 1977, while the maximum 130 lb men's world record is held by Jorge Potier with a massive 465 lb fish taken on 23 July 1976. While this area holds a grip on the world records, it should be noted that porbeagles over 400 lb have been landed from the Shetland Islands.

For numbers of porbeagles the Isle of Wight shark grounds must surely be best. In late June and early July, Gosport skipper Ted Legge has had some incredible sport for his clients, and in 1987 set a record with a haul of seventeen sharks in one day. All these were smaller fish and were returned for future sport. Initially, when these grounds were first discovered by Dick Downes and Trevor Prince, big fish to 300 lb were present. Then the overkill began and the decline in size and numbers. There followed a period when it was hardly worth trying for them, then slowly the fishing picked up.

Ted's dedication to locating the fish using his Decca equipment has made him the leading shark skipper in the UK. One of Ted's favourite methods for porbeagle is to freeline a livebait under the boat, a method I mentioned in the previous chapter. If ever a shark needed a livebait it is the porbeagle, and I have seen them ignore deadbaits lying in a rubby trail to rip a pollock off a set of feathers, or even take a whole string of coalfish. They don't seem as 'turned on' by a rubby trail as other species, but I imagine it must draw them to the livebaits. Often you can get a run as soon as you put a bait in the water, even before any rubby sack has been hung over the side.

While we have some of the biggest porbeagles in the world, we certainly don't have the monopoly on them. Montauk, New York, and Rhode Island both have fish to over 300 lb recorded, and this is the only other area in the world to threaten the British stranglehold over most of the line class world records. As our anglers become better equipped they are beginning to push up these world records, and there may even be a time when a British man or woman's name is against every single world record for porbeagle.

Porbeagles are seldom found in warm water, working up from

Go Fishing for Shark

Porbeagle sharks represent the biggest body of catchable 'big' sharks around our coast but they are sometimes difficult to locate. This was one of Britain's biggest Porbeagles and captor Rick Cotrell had the head mounted from his 450 lb odd fish landed off the North Devon coast.

about South Carolina on the eastern seaboard of the United States, to New York, then across to Scotland, down the west coast of Ireland and Wales, and on up the English Channel to the east, until they reach the Isle of Wight. Several have been reported in the North Sea, although to the best of my knowledge they have been commercial catches and not rod and line.

At one time porbeagles were confused with mako in identification. The best way to distinguish them is by the teeth. The porbeagle has smooth teeth with a tiny basal cusp on either side, which the mako doesn't have. They also have what is known as a small secondary caudal keel that is not found in the mako.

There is no recorded instance of this fat little shark ever being responsible for an attack on humans, and one assumes that this is because it lives in colder water. Many anglers think the colder water slows their metabolism down sufficiently to make them less fierce and

72

ferocious. However, I point out that there aren't many people swimming in the sea around the rocky coasts of Britain, and if we tipped in 10,000 swimmers, surfers and board sailors every day, then one day we would get an attack. I imagine from the power in that broad tail and its teeth, it would have little trouble in inflicting considerable damage to a swimmer if it set about it.

Porbeagles are a fine sportfish, and hopefully we shall see more smaller fish released. As for tackle, I see no reason to go higher than 50-lb test, and more often 30-lb test would be perfectly adequate. A few people fish ultra-light tackle in pursuit of world records, but as tiring a fish over a long period of time could hardly be termed sporting, I see no reason to drop below 30-lb test. That way you can put quite a bit of pressure on a fish and at least let him know you are there. Many light tackle buffs believe they lose many of their fish through the fish cutting the line on rocks. This is not true, they just don't understand what pressures are applied to a hundred yards of line when dragged in a belly through the water. It is the water friction drag acting upon the line that causes it to break, not being snagged around a rock. For this reason it is best to keep a light tackle shark on as short a leash as possible, and thereby minimise any belly in the line.

Mako

This shark is shrouded in more mystery than any other, and this is for two reasons. They are a superb scrapping shark, both in and out of the boat, and they are also comparatively rare, likely to turn up almost anywhere, at any time. When there were more shark boats working off the south-west of Cornwall and Devon, a couple of big makos a year were lost. Now I can't think of a capture for some years.

They are superbly shaped, streamlined and with a power in the tail that is almost frightening. I've seen a mako roped off three times on a flying and hand gaff, yet still break free! Occasionally they were taken by blue shark anglers out deep-drifting in forty fathoms of water. One of the inshore hotspots that they did frequent was the Manacles

73

Go Fishing for Shark

The Mako shark is probably the best fighting shark of all and superbly streamlined. English angler Mark Johnson travelled to Islamorada in the Florida Keys to land this beauty. He fished with the author aboard Capt. David Day's *Marlin Too*.

rocks and reefs off south Cornwall. Looe, in Cornwall, holds the British record with a 500-lb fish taken by Mrs. Joyce Yallop of Norwich on the shark boat *Lady Betty* skippered by Alan Dingle. I fished with Alan many times, mainly for pollock, and lost two mako on whole pollock while fishing with his son, Phil.

British Species

There are no strict rules about mako fishing in British waters. You simply have to go out there and try. Possibly the best chance of success will come to the angler livebaiting for porbeagle, and I feel that a rubby trail has little effect on a marauding mako, other than possibly stimulating him if he is in your area. Vibration and sight are what it is all about when mako fishing, and this was once illustrated to me when I took a couple of them while trolling. We had just completed a turn with the boat, which slows the lures and stops them streaming bubbles. As the boat straightens, the lures pick up speed and crash through the surface. At the peak of speed one of the lures got taken, and thinking I was tied to a marlin I applied heavy pressure. Imagine my surprise when I saw a mako at the back of the boat! Although they will take a bunch of fillets draped on a hook, they will often stay close to the boat without taking a bait. It may pay to dish out an extra helping of rubby mixture in an effort to make them take, but movement of bait is sometimes better. A sudden flash if you jerk on the bait is all you need to make them take when they are like this, so it will pay an angler fishing a deeper bait suddenly to wind in fast to make his bait rise, then slack off and drop it back to make it sink. It is a small pointer, but one that keeps your mind occupied with the job in hand, and definitely gets you the odd extra take or two. Makos love tuna. Big or small they are going to like a struggling tuna, especially if it is bleeding. Then they have both sight and smell stimulants turned on and can flash in to remove a chunk, or your whole tuna, in a couple of seconds.

They are a beautiful shark with a steel blue and silver side, merging into a wide underbelly. A big black eye, and that half-open mouthful of jagged teeth complete the picture. They have a reputation not only for being hard scrappers, but for leaping clear of the water. Some have been said to clear thirty feet, which is some height, but none of the makos I have caught have left the water until they were on the gaff. They actually don't taste bad when eaten, and have even been sold in some restaurants as swordfish, but it's their stamina and aggressiveness at boatside which is probably the main reason why few are tagged and released. It's a brave crewmate that leans down over the side to release a hook and clip a tag in a very live mako!

It's hard to illustrate the speed of these sharks, but they have been

Go Fishing for Shark

Graeme gets to grips with a near 100 lb Blue. Note the heavy-duty gloves to avoid the wire cutting into his hands. Never take wraps of wire around your hand without these gloves on. The shark could power away and you would lose a couple of fingers.

clocked at 30 knots, making them the fastest of all sharks, and capable of catching most pelagic fish.

A big mako has a prodigous appetite when sufficiently stimulated. The British record mako of 500 lb was reputed to have a 50-lb conger eel in its stomach, while a 720-lb male contained a whole 110-lb swordfish, intact except for the tail section! They can top 1000 lb in the world record listings, but most anglers regard the capture of a mako as an achievement in itself, and don't worry too much about the size.

In the fighting stages that turn of speed can leave you with a belly in the line, so keep it as tight as possible, but don't go too crazy. He's a powerful fish, and most of the fun starts at the boat. You'll need a little strength in reserve for then. I have seen a mako come in as docile as a trained dog on a lead. The mate grabbed the wire, maybe scratched him with the gaff, and you would have thought a cruise missile had dropped in three feet off the stern! I have no hesitation in saying they are the most dangerous sharks at boatside, and for that reason must be treated with the utmost respect.

Thresher

This fish is very fast, due to the long upper tail lobe which propels it through the water and allows for some fast about-turns. While the biggest British fish is around 300 lb, some people have hooked monsters they estimate might have weighed 600 lb, some off the back of the Isle of Wight, a favoured mark for these 'sea foxes'. The man who is undisputed king of the thresher world is Gosport skipper Ted Legge. If ever a man deserved to take a British record thresher it must be Ted. Yet inevitably however many he racks up during a season, Ted will be quite likely to see a complete novice from his own dinghy take a horrendous shark of 500 lb or more. That's fishing. If we all got what we thought we deserved there would be no fish left in the sea!

Ted has a special way of fishing for thresher shark, much of which is with small hooks and livebait, and understandably he is telling nobody about it. Many clients book with him just to get the chance of a thresher shark, so why give his competitors all his hard-earned secrets? Of course he is also out on the sea a lot more than other people, so the odds are greater that one of his charters will connect with a thresher. Even so, it would be difficult to go out and expect a thresher every time you tried. They feed on the surface, but I have the feeling they can also be taken near the bottom, especially at dawn or dusk. By all means fire a livebait down deep using a lead. Use something like a scad livebait which is much more hardy than a mackerel, and survives a run to the bottom a lot better. I did a little experimentation myself using a Cyalume-mini lightstick attached to the trace about a foot in front of a scad, and fished it deep on bright days, shallower on cloudy days. My theory was that it appears the scad is chasing the mini-lightstick, which in turn lights up the scad when fished over sixty feet deep. Threshers are strong visual feeders, and have a large eye, indicative of a depth or night feeder. As yet I've hooked nothing on the lightstick bait, but if someone does it every time they go, one day they will become attached to a thresher.

They have a very small mouth for their size so drop hook sizes to 4/0 and 6/0. Mustad hooks of this size are particularly strong, and when fished on outfits of 30 lb or less will never straighten out. I believe they may be found around our main summer mackerel shoals, or may even follow the whitebait shoals on which the bass feed. Obviously their mouths are too small to feed on 8-lb bass, and their teeth are not long, but I have noticed that they are either sighted or caught close to an area of good bass fishing. For that reason I think they chase brit, whitebait or sand eels. That long tail is used to 'ball up' the bait into a tight school, and not, as many would believe, to lash into a fish to stun it. There was even an account of a commercial shark skipper having his head lashed off completely by the tail of a flailing thresher shark! It's not uncommon to hear of sightings of leaping threshers, presumably trying to rid themselves of sea lice, and there is even an account of a thresher leaping into a small boat!

On a standard shark drift pick the smallest bait you can, maybe a 6 inch mackerel which you de-bone and thread onto a 6/0 Mustad hook. You can either freeline this, or attach a balloon, but don't blow it up too big, just about the size of a large orange, and sufficient to support the bait. Thresher shark can be finicky, and will often mouth a bait before taking it. You can take them on heavy mono. I landed a

British Species

Prime bait for a day's sharking. A box full of mackerel, ready for the mincer or hookbait. Never be afraid to leave them a couple of days to soften if bad weather prevents you getting out. They will break down more easily then.

thresher of 130 lb on a deep-fished livebait in Mexico that was intended for marlin. It was on mono leader, and had only a few scuff marks from the teeth. Another tip is to wind in and drop back your bait in an effort to give it some movement. Anything that looks like an injured fish may promote a strike. If you livebait, do so by nicking a small hook like a 6/0 through the leading edge of a small mackerel or scad, then freeline it back under the boat with a small lead. The lead, say two ounces or so, can be fixed to the trace with a looped elastic band so that it breaks free.

Sharks like the thresher are still something of a rarity, and must be considered a prestige catch. But catch one on light tackle of 30-lb test or less, and you will have a scrap to keep your memories alive during the winter months in front of the fire!

79

Go Fishing for Shark

The author puts the pressure on one of the big bull sharks he hooked using a flank of Amberjack. The tail of a 300 lb shark is seen sticking out by his feet. 'I need a bigger boat!' the author declared.

Warm-Water Sharks

In British waters the only real species of shark that we can honestly say is 'ours' is the porbeagle, that dumpy little predator that for some reason seems to have an affinity with our cold water. The other three, the blue, thresher and mako are true ocean wanderers and can be found worldwide. As well as these, there are dozens of other shark species lurking in the waters, from the lumbering great whale shark to neon-eyed sharks that scavenge the deep water of perpetual darkness. One shark which was caught off the French coast near Concarneau measured 26 feet and weighed four tons! Impressive, but hardly likely to have been landed on rod and line. Among the coral reef atolls of the warmer oceans are hives of small reef sharks, some no more than three feet in length, but among the most dangerous in the world to divers. They have an amazing speed and agility which is hard for the eye to follow. The following are some of the better fighting sharks that the angler can catch on rod and line.

Dusky Shark

This is a very powerful shark that has long been responsible for damage to commercial fishermen's lines, nets and even fish traps. They are large, up to and over 450 lb in weight, but are longer in the body than say the portly porbeagle. While fat sharks are always dogged fighters, I always have a little more respect for the skinny fish, as they have the power to whip round and grab something in a second.

They tend to feed near the bottom at night, but of course are not averse to rising to whatever water depth has the food. One dusky I took in Florida was on a deep-baited jig over three hundred feet deep, and that fish was nearly 200 lb! I like the shape of a dusky. As a bass has the perfect 'fishy' shape, so the dusky looks like a mean shark. Use a fairly chunky bait. A whole 10-lb bonito (skipjack tuna) impaled on a double hook rig and with both flanks cut open to release blood and give a flutter effect as the boat rises and falls. It can also be successful if you jig this bait hard, as they can be lured into striking even when they aren't too hungry. They are good fighters, but take them on nothing less than 50-lb test, as your bait is going to demand a lot of line before you get to strike in the first place. If you fish over rock, then use the 80-lb test. The extra power will stop them cutting you off on the rocks.

The Bronze Whaler

I have no idea how large these grow, and little fishing information is available for them. That they can be aggressive was illustrated to me while marlin fishing off Cabo San Lucas, on the Baja peninsula. We were filming a commercial that demanded some underwater close-up action of a marlin in the water. I had brought in a 250-lb blue marlin on a lure and while he still had colour, the film crew dropped into the water. They bounced right back again shouting that the ocean was full of sharks, circling beneath the marlin they were trying to film. They decided it was a lot safer to film surface shots on this one, and save the underwater stuff for the next marlin I caught. All the time that marlin must have been giving out good vibrations, as a pack of whalers circling deep began to rise in the water as they gained confidence. Filming would soon be over, but suddenly one of the whalers moved in and hit the marlin full on, taking a semi-circular chunk out near the marlin's tail. All aboard were impressed with the performance, and we took the blue in to port, rather than release it to the sharks.

The following day we ran to the same spot, which was the Jamie Bank some way offshore. Again the water was alive with mackerel, marlin and bronze whalers. Our back-up boat, the *Bacardi* captained

Warm-Water Sharks

The sleek lines of the shark can be seen by the author's fish coming near the boat. The split-tail mackerel bait can still be seen hanging from the jaws.

Go Fishing for Shark

by Carlos Cosa fished for striped marlin to pass the time as they waited for the film crew. What they hooked was a broadbill swordfish, and after a two-man fight it was chopped to pieces by the 'bronzies'. The rest of that day was spent trying to get a live caballito bait down past the sharks to the marlin. Several times we hooked up on sharks that hit the baits, and once I had a striped marlin that I could see in the water, but which would not come up through the sharks that circled ominously near the surface. As we needed the fish fresh, we put a second man on the rod and eventually persuaded him up to where the cameramen tentatively shot their footage with one eye through the viewfinder and the other on the bronze whalers! They seem to congregate wherever the pickings are easy, and the fish we hooked ran to around 150 lb. All gave a good account of themselves on 30-lb test, and I would think that chumming over an offshore bank would bring them up for the baits.

Whitetip Sharks

There are two types of whitetip shark, the reef whitetip shark and the ocean whitetip shark. The latter is much larger and runs to over 600 lb. The largest I have a photograph of is a 300-pounder. They work the same grounds as the bonito and tuna, obviously feeding on the tuna when they ball up whitebait on the surface, and they lose all their caution in the feeding frenzy. There is no way under normal conditions that a whitetip will have the horsepower to catch a bonito in full flight. Bonito move like aquatic bullets!

The best way to take them is by slow-trolling with a live tuna, not too big, about 10 lb in weight, bridle-rigging it through the front of the eye sockets. Faced with trolling like this with two dead and one livebait, they always seem to go for the livebait. Smaller reef whitetips have a habit of chopping baits in half if you troll too close to the reef. The best way to overcome this is to run a 'stinger' hook near the tail of the bait which will be a nice surprise for the next whitetip that decides to take a chop.

The ocean whitetips will pack together when the feeding is good, especially during the late March tuna run of yellowfins off the Indian Ocean island of Mauritius. Sometimes the radio crackles as skippers

Warm-Water Sharks

The Whitetip shark grows to a good size and follows the bonito shoals, moving in when a feeding frenzy makes the bonito lose their caution. They have a big jaw-frame, armed with several rows of serrated teeth.

up and down the Le Morne trolling drop-off tell of the number of whitetips in the water. They have a good, wide set of jaws, not unlike the tiger and have no difficulty in securing a bonito whole. I have heard of them being taken deep, but generally they can be located up near the surface, where their piggy small eyes search out food. A good fighter, it can go crazy at the gaffing stage, so take care.

Hammerhead Shark

The most easily identified of all the sharks, due to that strange anvil-like head, at the extreme end of which the eyes are located. They are known man-eaters, though the chances are remote of ever being bitten by any shark if you use common sense. Hammerheads grow big, certainly to 1000 lb, though I would guess a 150-lb fish is average. They are very strong scrappers, long and lithe in form, with an enormous dorsal fin, far larger for its size than any other shark. When initially sighted swimming free on the surface they can be particularly difficult to bait. I assume this is because they have fed the night or day previously, and are merely swanning on the surface taking a quick suntan!

A freshly killed, disembowelled tuna can make their mind up, but generally you catch then when you least expect them to show. When they are sufficiently stimulated they will hit anything. I've seen them bite the propeller, hull and gaff heads, so make sure you have a nice fresh bait. I believe that most of them come when surface fishing with either trolled or drifted baits, but I have taken them at over 200 feet while fishing out of Islamorada on the old shark boat *Ace* with Capt. Jim Taylor. On those occasions we used concrete blocks tied to the hook bend with dacron to hold the bait down against the force of the Gulf Stream. Off Miami they regularly take fish from 100 to 200 lb while fishing the wrecks, as the hammerhead often decides to take part in events and rips smaller fish off the hooks as fast as the customers hook them.

Hammers, although primarily ocean fish, will come into shallow water, and I have heard accounts of them showing up in the deeper channels that tarpon fishermen use. That wide head gives them an excellent range of smell location so they don't need a lot of scent to

The strange anvil-like head is the unmistakable hallmark of the Greater Hammerhead shark. The author took this fish on a surface fished skipjack tuna.

hunt down their prey. They are a nicely formed shark, that high dorsal, big broad tail, and tapered muscle body gives them both speed and power. It is rare to see them in packs, generally they are in ones and twos, unless something particularly succulent is in the area, like a dead whale carcass, when you will see several. When scouting near the bottom they also have a taste for skates and stingrays. Specimens of hammerheads that have been caught have had the barbs of stingrays embedded in their snouts and chins!

Hammerheads were once popular as a commercial fish with the liver, hide and fins all being used. One of the best fish to take on both 50-lb and 30-lb outfits, the hammerhead will give you a workout you won't forget. There are two types, the common and the great hammerhead. As the difference is of purely theoretical interest to the shark fisherman, and both species are scrappers, there is little point in detailing it.

Tiger Shark

These grow big, and they have an appetite for grabbing anything that gets in their way! They top 1300 lb and some people believe they might go over 2000 lb. Even a 300-lb tiger has a set of jaws that send a shiver down the spine, and those jaws are full of serrated edged teeth—almost like having 150 razor blades in your mouth!

Tiger sharks are a sort of refuse collector of the piscine world. If they can get it down their throats they don't worry too much what it tastes like. The tigers I have landed though have had a preference for amberjacks or whole 20-lb yellowfin tuna. As I said, they have a big appetite with teeth to match.

They love really warm water and can be taken close to shore as well as out deep. The cooler the water gets, the less your chance of finding one, but they will tolerate temperate oceans and seas from time to time. Australia hosts some of the biggest tigers in the world, but it's the Indian Ocean that is thought to hold the largest, presumably because it is also the warmest ocean in the world. This means there is a lot of unexpected tiger territory for the shark angler, as the east coast of Africa is one of the most underfished places in the world. A serious effort somewhere off Kenya, Tanzania or Mozambique is

Warm-Water Sharks

Capt. Jim Taylor and his deckmate have their hands full as they bring aboard one of the author's 400 lb Tiger sharks. Fish this size can be very dangerous and should be handled with respect.

liable to produce the really big one to approach or perhaps top, that magic 2000-lb mark.

They are almost certainly at the top of the man-eating lists, together with the great whites, as a tiger has little or no fear once it has been stimulated into feeding mode. Tigers attack boats, people, even sea lions, and do their best to swallow all as those razor-sharp teeth do their job. The cuts a big tiger makes on another fish would do a surgeon's knife proud!

They need a lot of food to keep them happy, so you should either fish with the biggest chum slick you can shovel overboard, or fish an area they are known to frequent in their search for food. Offshore banks and reefs always house a resident population of big food fish in the 20 -- 50 lb range, so they are good hunting grounds. They will be found in the vicinity of submerged wrecks closer to shore, as they cash in on whatever is going at the time. In the Florida Keys there are many such wrecks, stretching all the way down from West Palm Beach to Key West, the bottom of the Florida Keys chain. Tigers from 200 lb right on up to 1000 lb are both seen and caught on whole amberjacks that visit the area in early spring for spawning. They can be taken on a bait near the bottom, or right at the surface, particularly if you have the good fortune to find the carcass of a whale or porpoise floating. They love mammal meat, which is a shame, but then that's the chain of survival in nature.

Big tigers will give you a hard time, with the occasional long run, and long periods of stalemate when the tail fin just throbs away. Keep the pressure on though and you can get them. The answer is to keep a constant pressure on the rod, winding down hard whenever the tip starts to straighten from the horizontal. A tiger is one of the biggest sharks you are likely to catch, and impressive when he nears the wireman, showing those dark stripes on the brown flanks that give him his name.

Bull Shark

This is another tropical shark that fits into the 'big' category. Probably topping 800 lb, they have a cavernous mouth full of cutting teeth. Sometimes known as the Zambesi shark they have been linked numerous times with attacks on humans, especially in the vicinity of river mouths. They have no qualms at all about swimming up a freshwater river for several miles, and will even attack people there.

This species likes the same hunting grounds as the tiger, often nipping in before them to whack a lump of flesh from a big amberjack. The tiger cleans up of course, but treat bulls the same as you would a tiger. Use a big bait, preferably still bleeding, either a live amberjack or an entire flank. Invariably the bull shows up when you are happily engaged in the capture of some other smaller sporting species, and decides to take part in the fun. Therefore if you have your shark rod ready you can pop on the remains of the bait he has hit and drop it straight back to him. A take should follow shortly.

Big bull sharks in excess of 200 lb or so should be treated with respect. They are dogged fighters, often staying deep, so you will have

Warm-Water Sharks

Beautiful in the water, sharks like this 300 lb fish have a lot of power left at the boatside. Care should be exercised in wiring up any shark, whether it is to be released or brought aboard.

to use the benefit of a good shoulder harness to start lifting them up. Take short pumps with the rod, and fast turns with the reel handle, gaining line whenever you can. They also have a preference for small tuna in the 10-lb range which you can bump across the bottom using a piece of concrete or iron attached about 30 feet from the hookbend. That way, should the weight get snagged on the bottom you can break it out using the boat's engines and still have your trace and hook intact. For both tigers and bull sharks I would not advise coming down even to 50-lb class, as you may hit a 200-lb fish, but it could be 800 lb! Better to use the 80-lb or 130-lb outfits, and at least have a little say in the matter when your bait gets taken. The only time I would use a set of 50-lb would be if the shark has been chummed within visual range and the size and bulk can be successfully gauged. Even then I think most of you will reach for the 80-lb when you see the width across the back of the head!

Great White Shark

The only time I have fished for great white sharks was on an afternoon off Cape Town in South Africa. It was something of a half-hearted affair and being stationed only some three hundred yards off a popular beach, with a sandwich bait of dogfish and bluefish, you will appreciate my misgivings. A few commercials were handlining a reef nearby. We caught nothing, which was what I expected, despite being told that this had been a dangerous place to swim in years gone by. The following day one of the commercials had their outboard attacked by a rogue great white, about 100 yards from where we had been fishing! I was just in the right place at the wrong time!

That episode only serves to illustrate the unpredictability of this, the world's most efficient, fearless killing machine. A rare species, they are reputed to run as high as 5000 lb, second only to megaladon, which could have swallowed a car in one gulp. The Great Barrier Reef, Dangerous Reef, and the south of Australia host some fearful whites, yet they have also been caught off New York to 3400 lb. Most are harpooned, but they can be enticed to feed, generally by chumming with mammal meat such as whale. However this means instant disqualification of a catch should you take a world record fish, as mammal meat is not allowed.

They can be quite shy when they first arrive in a chum slick, and a bait should only be dropped back to them when they have gained confidence in feeding. There then comes a time when they actually get too confident in feeding and start taking bites out of anything in the water. With their great strength hidden beneath their bulk it is not surprising that they have actually sunk some boats.

All in all I rate the chance of finding one as minimal, the chance of landing one even less. However, the central Atlantic archipelago of the Azores has seen several huge whites, especially when they ran the whaling station off Pico. Richard Hatch, an Aussie who is running a marlin boat there, believes that the instinct to go to the whaling station is inherited by the progeny of this great shark, and he planned to experiment by dropping drums of chum in the main channel from where the whaling station was, over a long period of time. Through the days and weeks the smell from those drums would ooze out into the ocean currents, beckoning the great whites that wander in search of food. Their inherent knowledge of the old whaling station, together with the constant scent trail of fish blood would help Richard to catch one of these great sharks. I don't think the idea is far-fetched—as I have said earlier, a similar idea was tried for porbeagles by a Plymouth man out in deep water. I have yet to hear back from Richard Hatch, but I guess he has as much chance of taking a 2000-lb white as anyone, especially with his previous knowledge of big fish from Australian waters. As for tackle, there is no point in playing tag with these fish. It has to be the maximum set of 130-lb test, with plenty of it on the spool, and when you get to the gaffing stage, I wish you the very best of luck. You'll need it!

Other Sharks

There are almost 200 species of sharks, and there is a chance you may stumble across one of them, so I give here a few of the others.

The lemon shark is thought to be responsible for attacks on humans, and can run to over ten feet in length which puts it in the 'big' category. It has pale yellow sides and is pretty light in overall colour shading which gives rise to its name. They love warmer water and will often run into bays, creeks and flats, which can make them a target for the 'skinny water' sharkman. Do not wade near them though, they can be unpredictable and dangerous. It is a good scrapping shark on the light to medium tackle range. The largest two I landed were 300 and 350-lb sharks from the mouth of the Gambia river in West Africa.

The silky shark grows to eight or ten feet and is caught offshore in deeper water. They have a reputation as racers, and can peel line off a big reel once they get going. Line of 50-lb class should be sufficient.

Blacktips are primarily a shallow-water species that are thought to

Go Fishing for Shark

Three's a crowd! The author set the Gambia alight only last year when he boated these two huge Lemon sharks of 300 and 350 lb aboard a small open boat. They were landed a short distance from the Atlantic Hotel, near the Banjul River.

grow over eight feet long. I have never seen one on the flats that large, but three feet would be a good average. They also sport the nickname 'spinner' shark amongst the flats fishermen, as they race off when hooked, then spin and roll trying to throw the hook. A definite light tackle shark, so chase it on 12 lb outfits.

The brown shark is very similar to the bronze whaler of the Pacific, and it may even be the same species, or a subspecies, much like the Pacific and Atlantic marlins and sailfish. It is a good scrapper, usually encountered while chumming offshore and you can get more than one in the chum line at a go. They are known to run inshore snaffling the surf fisherman's bait intended for striped bass or red drum. Invariably they break the line, but at least it gives the surf fisherman a story of the one that got away! They are a size that can be taken on 30 lb and 50 lb, but care should be exercised when they are brought into the boat, as they have an aptitude for reincarnation as makos!

Warm-Water Sharks

Going solo means hooking, playing then boating a shark single handed. While it could be deemed dangerous on a Mako, it can be fun on Blues and small Porbeagles.

Those are the sharks that you are most likely to take. To me, possibly one of the greatest challenges lies in pinning a really big bait down deep on somewhere like the Azores or Condor bank with a big weight. There are some massive deep-water sharks about that run over the 1000-lb mark, it's just that nobody has yet perfected a technique for fishing them. It's a big ocean even on the surface, but you can barely imagine what is going on down there in that deep black water where light seldom penetrates. It is the last avenue of pioneering for the modern shark fisherman.

Conservation

Any shark angler who takes this sport seriously must give adequate thought to putting as many fish back as possible. While most of the shark species are under little or no commercial fishing pressure, there are benefits to fishermen in returning them. I am not one of those anglers who bursts into tears when a shark is brought in. There are plenty of sharks about, especially in tropical waters, and I have little sympathy with the extremists in conservation. If you want to keep a shark for proper weighing and photographs, then do so. What must surely be wrong however, is the wholesale slaughter of shark after shark, for there can be no real glory in seeing yourself beside a pile of ten blue sharks. It is better to get a good picture of your biggest of each species, on different types of tackle, and return any under that weight. A returned shark can not only give the chance of that surge of excitement to another angler, but you may even catch the same fish years later when it is a lot larger. Of course there is the view that you are only putting a shark back to see it caught by a Japanese longliner. Although this may happen I feel it is morally wrong to destroy something which has no use to you, or anyone else. If the shark killed is subsequently eaten, or some part of it utilised, then it is a different matter. Certainly keeping the odd big shark or two doesn't keep me awake at night, but it seems common sense to try and return most of the undersized fish.

Conservation

The author has regularly helped with the tagging of blue shark using the Irish Tourist Board tags. Returns from tagged fish have shown they roam up to 2000 miles from point of capture.

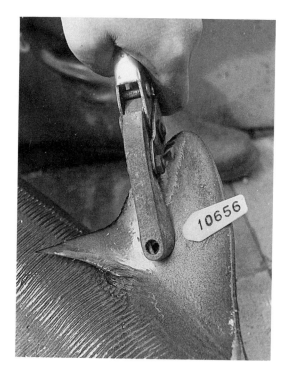

There are several research programmes in operation throughout the world. Here in the UK a tagging programme was conducted from the port of Plymouth. Many blue sharks were killed at that time, and they provided ideal specimens for dissection. At first it was thought that many of the blues didn't feed when they came in British waters, as a high percentage of the sharks dissected had little or no stomach content. Then it was learned that during a fight a shark will throw its stomach literally inside out in an effort to dislodge the hook, which accounted for the empty stomachs! Many fish were also tagged and released, and recaptures revealed startling statistics on the migratory movement of the blue. It was found that they were split into two different groups, with males on one side of the Atlantic and females on the other. The Montauk area of New York on the eastern seaboard of the United States had one population, while we had the other. Presumably they meet up somewhere for reproduction

97

purposes, but as yet no area has been pinpointed. Perhaps it is good that nobody knows, because once the breeding areas are known, the species would be subject to over-fishing. The British tagging programme has finished, but the Central Fisheries Board (CFB) in Ireland still run one, and have statistics showing that the blues tagged and released from their major sharking ports travel south across the Atlantic to the coast of Spain, Portugal and North Africa, as well as the central eastern Atlantic Ocean. The proliferation of blues during our summer months when the North Atlantic Drift is closest to the southern shores, enables many fish to be tagged. The more we tag, the greater the chance of a subsequent recapture which then provides migratory and growth information.

There are too few thresher or mako sharks caught to tag, but the porbeagle is known to be a localised shark, and will not travel the same distances as the blue. A coldwater shark, it is therefore more likely to suffer from overfishing, so we desperately need more porbeagles to be tagged and released. One fish tagged off Ireland was caught several years later from exactly the same area, indicating their preference to stay localised. The CFB supply data sheets on which information is logged, plus a leather punch and supply of plastic cattle-style tags with details and tag number printed on.

In the United States they take the idea of conservation much further and the information supplied by both the NMFS and the US Department of Commerce co-operative shark tagging programme is the most sophisticated anywhere. As well as fin tagging with either Jumbo Rototag, or the 'dart' style tag, they have been injected with an antibiotic that marks their vertebrae. A cross-section of shark vertebrae is the best way to age a fish and provides interesting data. Angler participation with the NMFS co-operative shark tagging programme began in 1963. A hundred recreational fishermen were selected to field-test tags, and evaluate different feasibility projects to tag large and potentially dangerous sharks. Interest and participation expanded over the next few years, although in most instances sharks tagged by their own marine biologists from commercial vessels were not assigned to the 'commercial' category. Between 1963 and 1983 the percentage of tagging effort broke down as follows: commercial fishermen 4%, NMFS biologists 17%, other biologists 17%, foreign fish observers 10% and anglers 52%. This gives an indication of the assistance we can give researchers in the field of tagging sharks.

In this same time period, covering many different species including swordfish, they tagged 53,252 fish with 1703 recaptures from 47 different species tagged. The longest distance travelled in miles was 3630, and the maximum miles per day travelled was 27. The longest time that any blue shark was at liberty after tagging was 6 years. Another tagged off New York ran south covering 1714 miles in 64 days and was recaptured off Venezuela. Twenty-one of the 885 recaptured from the western Atlantic Ocean releases were subsequently recaptured in the eastern Atlantic. Two of the 46 recaptures from eastern Atlantic releases were recaptured in the western Atlantic.

The NMFS have all records computerised for ease of access, and the western Atlantic distribution of blues makes interesting reading. Beginning in April or May, large numbers of blues begin moving from the Gulf Stream toward North Carolina, to the offings of Newfoundland. They are most common on the continental shelf and the Grand Banks throughout the summer. During this summer period they can be found in water as shallow as 100 feet off New York and southern New England. The blues remain well offshore during periods of low salinity caused by freshwater run-off from the Hudson River and Delaware and Chesapeake Bays. I wonder if any substantial run-off from somewhere like the huge River Shannon system in western Ireland could affect the salinity of the water inshore, bearing in mind that the 100-foot mark (16 fathoms) can be very close to shore. The catch is heavily dominated by males, and most blues mature when about six years old (approximately 7 feet). In late summer and autumn most of the blue sharks begin moving south and offshore, but the migration routes are not clearly defined. They have been reported through water temperature ranges of 8–27°C or 46–81°F.

It has been discovered in tropical areas of the western Atlantic Ocean that blues submerge to cooler subsurface water layers. Our own eastern Atlantic distribution also shows a north–south migration that is related to size and sex. Returns from tagged blues released in the Canary Islands and off the Cape Verde Islands show that some blues travelled northward along the African and European coasts over distances of at least 1600 miles. It appears that the Mediterranean serves as a nursery ground where young are born and remain during the first years of their life. This is apparent from the size of blues taken off the tourist venues on the Algarve coast (either 5-lb blues or large 200-lb females). I also believe that the extreme eastern Mediterranean is a nursery ground for the giant bluefin tuna. This water also holds a huge population of sardines, and both are easy for an immature predator to catch, and of high nourishment value.

Results of other tagging studies in the eastern Atlantic suggest that there are two main movements of blues off south-west England: an initial arrival of females at the start of the season, with more males following from the end of July to August. Tag returns show the blue sharks move south during September, and my own experience from catching them indicates that this is the best time for blue shark fishing. Many big 100-lb specimens have been taken in both Ireland and England during October. I am sure the water temperature has not peaked by mid-August, but is still rising until September, depending on the strength and direction of the North Atlantic Drift. Even if the weather turns cold in September, it will take longer for the water temperature to drop than is normally thought. I also believe the blues push far up to the north of Ireland, and this has been borne out by catches of blues from as far north as County Donegal, while blues from the mainland of England are rarely caught north of the Bristol Channel. Thus the big blues usually caught in October may be those returning in a southward direction along the western Atlantic coast of Ireland, en route to the Mediterranean or the coast of west Africa.

It appears from the information received that the blues can travel the Atlantic in an east–west direction as well as vice versa. Results of some of the blue sharks tagged off Irish waters gave three such transatlantic crossings. Two were recaptured off New York after 364 and 412 days respectively, while a third was recaptured near Barbados after $3^1/2$ years. Two blues tagged off England also moved to waters off New York. It is thought the blues may use or be carried by the major current systems over the entire Atlantic basin. This would support my own theory that the very lowest in the food chain

Conservation

The author looks a bit ragged after battling out this big Blue taken late in the season out of Courtmacsherry in Southern Ireland. Wired and gaffed aboard alone, fish of this size are worthy adversaries. The author believes Southern Ireland gives better sport with sharks late in September when specimen Blues and Porbeagles can be taken. The North Atlantic Drift keeps temperatures high until early October.

affect the final predator link in how far the major ocean currents may change each year. The average surface current speed over a roughly circular route from North America across to Africa and then back to the Caribbean to connect with the Gulfstream is about 0.65 knots. This gives a fish drift factor of 15.6 miles per day and covers the course in 609 days. Of course any swimming motion on the shark's part would boost this drift factor considerably.

Sonic tracking experiments demonstrated that the average swimming speed of sharks was less than one knot, although in an issue in the 1986 Overview newsletter of the Shark Tagger summary, there is a report of a mako shark that set a new speed record of 36 miles per day. The prevailing currents and the international extent of blue shark captures have indicated that they may be all of a single stock, rotating continually, using these intercontinental ocean currents. Without co-operation from anglers, scientists and biologists, such information would not become known, and therefore we would not appreciate how an existing fish stock should be handled.

Other bits of information make you realise how much more could be learned about a species if we tagged and released more. Three sandbar sharks were recaptured after a staggering 20 years of freedom. A sandbar actually lived for 21.3 years before being caught again. A blue shark travelled from the Azores into the Mediterranean, a distance of over 1000 miles. In 1985 a record number of sharks were tagged (7100), and some 251 were recaptured. The first tagged blue shark crossed the equator into the southern hemisphere after release in the western Atlantic. A tagged sandbar shark was examined after 17 years of liberty, and was still found to be immature. All these snippets illustrate the importance of what I have said about doing our best to protect our future.

Much of this information is related to the blue, but as I have said, we should be considering compulsory tagging for the porbeagles, which unlike the blue, may be present all year.

Any shark that has the chance of bringing in cash on a fishmonger's slab draws the interest of the commercial fishing fraternity. Intensive commercial fisheries always deplete stocks in a far more devastating way than rod and line fishing. What will stop this devastation is not legislative controls. Policing and enforcing

Conservation

such laws is difficult if not impossible. The only thing that will stop commercial fisheries is for the species to get so close to extinction that fishing for it ceases to become viable. Anglers often think they have done the damage, and they obviously contribute to a lesser extent. But what the popularisation of a type of sport fishing actually does is direct the attention of the commercial community to that species. And they are hardly interested in fishing for sport, where the fish has a chance to win.

There used to be a longline fishery for porbeagle sharks in the western north Atlantic around 1960, primarily by Norwegians. In 1964 annual catches increased from 1800 tons to 9300 tons, then declined dramatically to about 200 tons. Growth to maturity in a porbeagle takes about six to nine years and only four young are born under normal conditions. The slow growth rate and low reproductive potential coupled with mass overfishing will see such a sharp decline in a porbeagle fishery anywhere.

Many shark fishermen now openly refuse to charter a boat captain that sells the sharks as a financial sideline, and who is not interested in future sport. I say again if you keep the odd shark, that's fine, but extreme care should be exercised. If I catch a huge porbeagle, tiger or blue I will, like any angler, claim a record, but to keep killing every fish knowing full well that it is neither a record, nor your personal best on that tackle, is to play dangerously with your own future sport and that of others. The apex chain of predators, those at the top that all anglers dream of catching, have commercial overkills, high PCBs and pollutants, and baitfish biomass reductions to live through as well as us fishermen. The one consolation we can offer is that given proper approaches and remedies to these problems, by acting now there may just be a slim chance that sharks will be swimming to be caught by the anglers of the future. So keep shaking that rubby bag!

GO FISHING FOR

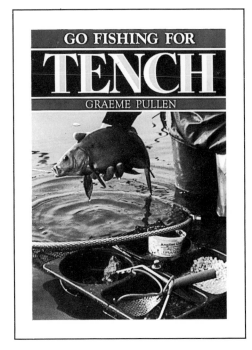

All available in the same series at £9.95 each.

96pp, 240 x 172mm
16pp colour and approx. 30 black & white photographs.